Foundations of Education

DANTES/DSST* Test Study Guide

All rights reserved. This Study Guide, Book and Flashcards are protected under the US Copyright Law. No part of this book or study guide or flashcards may be reproduced, distributed or stored in a retrieval system, or transmitted in any form or by any means, electronic, mechanical, photocopying, recording, or otherwise, without the prior written permission of the publisher Breely Crush Publishing LLC.

© 2026 Breely Crush Publishing, LLC

*DSST is a registered trademark of Prometric and its affiliated companies, and does not endorse this book.

97105122043

Copyright ©2003 - 2026, Breely Crush Publishing, LLC.

All rights reserved.

This Study Guide, Book and Flashcards are protected under the US Copyright Law. No part of this publication may be reproduced, distributed or stored in a retrieval system, or transmitted in any form or by any means, electronic, mechanical, photocopying, recording, or otherwise, without the prior written permission of the publisher Breely Crush Publishing, LLC.

Published by Breely Crush Publishing, LLC
10808 River Front Parkway
South Jordan, UT 84095
www.breelycrushpublishing.com

ISBN-10: 1-61433-694-6
ISBN-13: 978-1-61433-694-5

Printed and bound in the United States of America.

*DSST is a registered trademark of Prometric and its affiliated companies, and does not endorse this book.

Table of Contents

Past and Current Influences *1*
    A Brief History of Colonial Education *1*
    Freud *3*
    Piaget *3*
    Vygotsky and ZPD *5*
    John Dewey *6*
    Benjamin Bloom *8*
    Schools of Thought *9*
    Democratic Ideals *9*
    NEA and NCLC *12*
    Cardinal Principles of Secondary Education *12*
    Brown v. Board of Education *14*
    No Child Left Behind Act *15*
    Kindergarten *17*
    Single Salary Schedule *18*
    Social Rights Movement *19*
    Religion in School *19*
    A Nation at Risk *21*

Contemporary Issues *22*
    Equity *22*
    Gifted Children *24*
    Title IX *26*
    Governance *27*
    Department of Education *28*
    State Board of Education *28*
    School Board *29*
    School District *29*
    Teachers' Union *30*
    Curriculum *32*
    John Dewey and John Bobbitt *33*
    ESSA *34*
    Common Core *35*
    Values Centered Curriculum *36*
    Social-Emotional Learning *37*
    Metacognition *38*
    Multiple Intelligences *39*
    Learning Styles *40*
    Scaffolding *41*
    Differentiated Instruction *42*

- Carnegie Unit 43
- Professional Issues 44
- Alfred Binet and Intelligence Testing 45
- Standardized Testing 47
- Professional Judgment 48
- Zero Tolerance Policies 49
- Technology Issues 51
- Partnership for 21st Century Skills 51
- Digital Divide 53
- Technology in Learning 55
- Remote Education 57

Contemporary and Past Issues 58
- Tradition and Progress 58
- Standardized Tests 59
- National Versus Local Control 61
- Education Policy 62
- Secular Versus Religious 63
- Widmar v. Vincent 65
- Wisconsin v. Jonas Yoder 65
- Public Versus Private 66
- Montessori School 66
- Private School 68
- Charter Schools 69
- Vouchers 70
- Civil Rights 70
- Admission Preferences 72
- Indian Child Welfare Act 72

Sample Test Questions 74
Test Taking Strategies 108
What Your Score Means 108
Test Preparation 109
Legal Note 109

PAST AND CURRENT INFLUENCES

 A Brief History of Colonial Education

Learning is a huge part of human life. From the moment we are born, we begin learning about the world around us. Though we often learn the basics of walking and talking from our families, most people will also spend a considerable portion of their early lives in the education system in some manner. The average North American child will spend between eleven and fourteen years at school.

While the essential building blocks of formal education—instruction and assessment—haven't changed much over the last hundred years or so, the ways in which we approach their implementation have. In order to fully understand the contemporary issues being discussed in education today, it's important to briefly look back to the first colonial schools in the United States and explore their purposes and struggles. We will also explore the philosophies, theories, and ideologies that helped shape the education system into what it is today so that we can understand where the current policies and issues originated and consider how we might approach them in the future.

In the seventeenth and eighteenth centuries, education looked very different from today's system, varying substantially depending on how wealthy a child's family was, which colony they lived in, and which religious tradition they followed. Regardless, education most often started at home where basic reading and writing were taught by the child's mother or, if they could afford one, a tutor or nanny. Before the Revolution, parents in the Southern colonies continued to employ tutors for their children while schoolhouses and church schools were becoming popular in the New England and middle colonies. These were called common schools because all of the students, regardless of their age, sat together in a one-room schoolhouse and were taught by a single teacher.

Boys typically received more education than girls but both were allowed to attend school, though some schools were gender-segregated. Before the nineteenth century, there were very few formal secondary schools so most children would finish primary schools and start into vocational training, Latin schools, or college, or contribute to the family industry. Many states quickly adopted the practice of making separate, and eventually public, schools for students aged fourteen through eighteen in the 1800s following a number of legislative changes in Massachusetts. Early colonial education was very pragmatic in nature, with the idea being to give children the specific tools and skills they needed in life, which is why it varied so widely across the country. It also emphasized the importance of civic duty and morality, especially at church schools.

The first "textbook" most children learned from was the Bible. In addition to being more broadly available than traditional textbooks, children were familiar with many of the passages through prayer and worship, providing a foundation for literacy and understanding. However, many parents and schools also had formal textbooks brought over from England. Then came the first printing of *The New England Primer*, which quickly became the most popular teaching tool for the next century. After the Revolutionary War, Noah Webster's "blue-backed speller" took the spotlight because it organized different subjects and skills to be taught by age. Webster believed that children's ability to learn progressed as they grew and he organized his textbook to reflect this. Unsurprisingly, this idea laid the foundation for modern teaching materials as we will see when we look at Piaget's theory of cognitive development in the next section.

In 1837, Horace Mann was named secretary of the Massachusetts Board of Education and promptly undertook a significant overhaul of the education system and helped establish the first normal schools in the state. Normal schools were the first standardized teacher training programs in the U.S. They were already popular in Europe where they trained teachers for secondary and post-secondary schools but there was only one in the United States, and it had already closed in 1830.

Mann made it mandatory that teachers pass his re-established normal school if they were to be employed as a teacher at a Massachusetts public school. Previously, any high school graduate could leave their last day of class and walk into a primary common school to begin teaching the following day.

Mann was so passionate about teacher training and improving the quality of education that he actually delivered lectures at a number of normal schools, as well as started a biweekly education journal called *Common School Journal* so that teachers could stay updated on new education reforms and research.

Mann also fully supported the idea of public education and insisted that school be free for all to attend so that children of all backgrounds could receive a quality education. For Mann, education was in the public interest and it made sense for everyone to have access to it.

By 1870, all of the states had some form of publicly supported elementary education. At this time, the fields of child psychology and formal pedagogical research also began to grow. These two factors led to the landscape of education in America changing dramatically, thanks in large part to several key players and ideas that we will look at now.

Freud

The field of psychology quickly exploded after Freud published *The Interpretation of Dreams* in 1899, beginning the psychoanalysis craze which maintained in some forms all the way to the early 2000s. As more research was being done into the human mind and condition, many academics began to apply these new psychological concepts to education to see if it could be improved through understanding how children grow and think. This early research, and excitement surrounding the new field of study, led to some of the first pedagogical "fads" that swept the nation. **Pedagogy** refers to methods and strategies for teaching, typically in formal academic settings. Modern education and teacher training are focused heavily on pedagogy and practicing research-supported methods in the classroom, so it's important to know what theories and ideologies are behind some of the biggest trends and strategies.

Piaget

While observing his children learning about the world around them, Swiss psychologist Jean Piaget became curious about how a growing mind processes information. Piaget staunchly disagreed with the pervasive belief at the time that intelligence was fixed and that children were merely less-capable adults. His work determined that children did not think less or "worse" than adults, but rather that children just thought quite differently from adults. Not only do they have to learn many cognitive skills which adults take for granted, but they also have to develop mental structures to allow for information to be processed.

Through his work at the Binet Institute, he noticed that children most commonly gave incorrect answers to logic questions and wanted to know why. By running a series of tests and rigorous studies, he developed a model called the **Stage Theory of Cognitive Development** in the 1920s which outlined four distinct phases of learning that children experience from birth to age fifteen. It's important to note that the ages associated with the stages are merely suggestions for when the average child will reach them and not necessarily the absolute cut off. The stages are as follows:

1. **Sensorimotor Stage (birth to two years old):** Infants learn about and interact with their world via their senses and begin to notice that their actions have consequences (crying brings a caregiver, touching something makes it move). They don't understand the "why" of cause and effect relationships. They begin to realize they are separate from other people and objects, and they eventually understand object permanence (that objects still exist even when you cannot see them).

2. **Preoperational Stage (two to seven years old):** Children start to think symbolically and learn to use language to represent objects and basic concepts. They still struggle with logical deduction and seeing situations from another's perspective and are noticeably egocentric as a result. They practice these skills through playing pretend and consolidate their learning into their rapidly growing memory.

3. **Concrete Operational Stage (seven to eleven years old):** Logical thinking improves dramatically and children begin to understand concrete logical deductions, such as the concept of conservation. For example, if a ball of clay is split in half and one half is rolled into a long cylinder while the other is squashed flat, a child at this stage can identify that they are the same amount of clay despite one looking larger. They will also start using inductive logic, applying knowledge from one situation to another. They are better empathizers but still have difficulty with abstract concepts and hypothetical situations, relying on concrete information and understandings.

4. **Formal Operational Stage (twelve and up):** Adolescents and teens become more concerned with philosophical and hypothetical concepts such as morality, ethics, politics, and social-emotional issues. They can think in the abstract and engage with thought experiments and deductive logic. These new skills allow them to plan for the future and they seek more independence and responsibility.

Piaget theorized that all children will go through these stages and that all will do so in this order. This is because his focus was on cognitive development, and in order to perform higher order functions, children must have the prerequisite skills and understanding. However, he also explained that some children may never reach later stages due to physical trauma to the brain, developmental disabilities, or lack of opportunity and training (this applies to the formal operational stage in particular).

While his purpose in developing the Stage Theory was not to figure out how children learn, many of the concepts he introduced for his research had major impacts on education. **Schemas**, for example, are cognitive frameworks that help individuals figure out how to act and react in various situations. Schemas can act as mental shortcuts because our brains can take in a large amount of information and quickly categorize it under one of our schemas. They also present a potential issue because schemas also encompass biases and stereotypes which can cause us to react to something poorly and without proper consideration. An example of a schema is a child learning to identify different animals. If a child has a cat at home, they will learn the schema of "cat" early on: big ears, furry, tail, claws.

While watching TV, they see a lion on screen and say, "Kitty!" Although the lion does not perfectly match their existing schema, they integrate it through a process called **assimilation**. However, when this child sees a dog for the first time, especially if it's a small dog, they may call it a cat because many of its characteristics match the existing cat schema. Once they are corrected that what they're seeing is actually a dog, they will build a new "dog" schema. This process is referred to as **accommodation**, where they are adjusting their existing schema, often creating a new schema in the process. This is one way in which children's cognitive processes become more sophisticated.

Schemas influence education because they affect how quickly and effectively people learn. As mentioned, schemas allow us to think quickly because we already have an existing framework for the incoming information. This also works for new information which can be assimilated or accommodated more efficiently if the learner has a related schema. Schemas can also make it more difficult to acquire new knowledge if that knowledge contradicts an existing framework. For example, if a child has a pair of heterosexual parents who represent and enforce traditional masculine and feminine gender roles at home, then it may be difficult for that child to understand and accept a female classmate who would rather play with trucks and wear boys' clothes than play with dolls and wear skirts because this scenario doesn't fit within their existing schema of gender roles.

To Piaget, children's development had to meet certain checkpoints before learning could occur. He believed that learning and cognitive development occurred when an individual's experiences interacted with their thoughts and ideas, regardless of the influence of others. Although progression through stages can be assisted by outside forces, the majority of it occurs within the child as their own abilities improve and adapt. This is called **cognitive constructivism**, wherein meaning-making occurs primarily at the cognitive level.

 Vygotsky and ZPD

Lev Vygotsky, conversely, saw learning and cognitive development as not only inseparable from each other but also from the social context in which the development happens.

He subscribed to social constructivism, which theorizes that meaning-making and learning cannot happen without a significant social aspect. Vygotsky developed the theory of the **zone of proximal development (ZPD)**, which defines the cognitive and social space in which a child will best learn and grow.

At the center of the child's knowledge is what they can accomplish unaided. These are the skills and knowledge they have internalized and can use on their own. From there, it enters the Zone of Proximal Development where children will apply the existing knowledge to new situations through the guidance of adults or peer collaboration. Furthest away from the child are the things they cannot yet accomplish, even with guidance or support. This means that children need to have an active role in their education and cannot just be passive receivers of information. Vygotsky's theory was not very well-known in the West until it was translated from Russian in 1962. The idea of the ZPD was used by critics of the American education system to help establish a pedagogical approach called the **open classroom** which emphasized "learning by doing." Open classrooms were common by this point in British public elementary schools and were called **informal education**. Open classrooms found their way into American public education, heralded as the ideal cure-all the rigid and old system needed.

The first and most staunchly open classrooms had little to no formal lesson delivery, no standardized tests, and no prescribed curriculum. The classroom was arranged into a series of learning or interest centers that students investigated whenever they liked and could learn at their own pace. These stations included subjects like reading, art, science, and even math.

Teachers had a more hands-off role in an open classroom and would structure lessons and activities for individuals with specific needs or for small groups. When they weren't leading an activity, they would check up on students at each center and give guidance when necessary. Many schools took the open classroom a step further and did away with age grade assignments altogether, with teams of teachers managing different centers where students of a variety of ages could learn together. Some even built new buildings that were more like the old one-room schoolhouses of colonial times so that children could move from center to center in one large area.

As with most fads in education, open classrooms faced plenty of criticism from a number of experts who saw many examples of the open classroom ideology being followed more in spirit than in practice. In the late 1970s, as a result of the national divide over the Vietnam War and cultural backlash against the values movement of the late 60s and early 70s (covered in more detail in Social/Economic Influences) open classrooms in the public system practically disappeared. People once again began blaming public school for the nation's woes and lax education standards were cited as the problem. The ideology's impact on education cannot be denied, however, because many teachers, in elementary school in particular, still use some ideas from the movement, such as learning centers, in combination with more teacher-centered methods.

John Dewey

John Dewey was an American philosopher and psychologist in the late nineteenth and early twentieth centuries who was heavily involved in education reform and theory. He believed in democracy and asserted that a healthy democracy was the human ideal and could be achieved through robust and considered schools as well as an informed public opinion supported by active media and accountable politicians. He wrote extensively on education, pedagogical approaches, and learning. Dewey saw school as a place not only for learning skills and knowledge but of self-discovery and personal growth, and so encouraged student-centered approaches. Dewey died in 1952, before the open-classroom revolution, but his writings suggest he would have been one of its critics because he was wary of any approach that put the onus of learning too much on either the student or the teacher. Dewey's goal was to encourage finding systems that balanced the role of the teacher with that of the student because he believed that the child is the determining factor in "both the quality and quantity of learning" because their interests and prior knowledge determined what they paid attention to and how much effort they put into activities. Anyone who's tried to get a child of any age to do something they don't want to do can confirm just how important it is for the child to "buy into" the learning.

Dewey's ideas and concepts made him a prominent figure in the **pragmatism** school of thought. People who subscribe to pragmatism in education believe that school should be a practical means to an end that teaches students things useful for everyday life while encouraging interpersonal and intrapersonal development.

A popular teaching strategy today called **problem-based learning (PBL)** can trace its origins to Dewey's writings as it uses teacher knowledge of the subject matter to spark students' interest and encourage them to actively engage with a problem to solve it. This is very different from the **factory model school** that Dewey was critical of in his work. Factory model is a term used to criticize the sterile and passive approach to education that is prevalent in many classrooms even to this day (see the writings of Ken Robinson for more on factory models). The point is to evoke the image of a school as a mass-production facility meant to be as efficient as possible at turning out students who meet specific criteria: the designated set of skills and knowledge they demonstrate and with a certain degree of aptitude. For many teachers and schools, it was easier to apply a standard approach for every student and assess their success in the same way because it streamlined the process.

Unfortunately, this approach doesn't take into account learning differences, the needs of students not going directly into university or the labor force after high school, or how to encourage social-emotional growth and the development of ethical principles. To Dewey, the best way to fix this was to further improve teacher education and make the job a vocational profession, like doctors and lawyers, because teachers provide a social service that can be traced directly to societal progress and success.

This view was supported by a number of stakeholders and teacher training was constantly being updated as the landscape of education in America developed. Another proponent of teacher education was noted psychologist B.F. Skinner who, in his essay collection *The Technology of Teaching*, devoted an entire section to exploring why some teachers fail to adequately guide their students. The main issue, he states, is that many teachers have not been properly educated themselves and, because they do not understand how students learn best, tend to fall back on unhelpful practices such as relying on lecturing material, not adapting material to meet a student's current level, actively avoiding difficult interactions (such as failing to empathize with an emotional student), and not providing enough positive reinforcement.

Benjamin Bloom

As psychologists and pediatricians gained more knowledge about child development, education specialists became concerned with how to integrate this knowledge into teacher training and pedagogical strategies. People were debating more about what was important for children to learn, what was the responsibility of teachers and what was expected from parents, and how to best impart skills and knowledge to students of various ages and aptitudes.

From 1949 to 1953, Benjamin Bloom, an educational psychologist, chaired a series of conferences at which a collection of educators, psychologists, and other stakeholders developed a system by which learning could be broken down and categorized. The model they developed was called Bloom's Taxonomy. The idea was to create a taxonomy that would give people writing curriculum and lessons a concrete framework they could compare their content against and know which skill or knowledge targets they were hitting.

The most basic kind of knowledge is memorization. Even young children can memorize things and repeat it back to you, but they will not know what it means until their knowledge becomes more sophisticated. From there, children learn to apply that knowledge in new situations. For example, a child has a stool in the bathroom to reach the counter to brush their teeth.

They want something up high in a different room, so they go grab their bathroom stool to solve this new problem. A child will be able to analyze information and ideas in order to classify it in new ways and synthesize new understanding. Once they can do this, they learn how to properly justify an idea or position and use their knowledge in persuasive ways. The highest cognitive order is creating new work or knowledge themselves using all of the skills and knowledge they've built up to that point.

Unlike Piaget's stages of cognitive development, Bloom's taxonomy does not represent a necessary chronological hierarchy through which the learners will progress. Children do not need to understand in order to create, as demonstrated by what happens when you give a young toddler a crayon and piece of paper. Instead, the taxonomy represents the different kinds of knowledge and skill demonstration which helps educators develop comprehensive learning programs for their students.

Schools of Thought

Of course, these are just a few of the many theoretical and psychological frameworks used to talk about issues in education. Before we look at some other perspectives in more detail, here are brief summaries of three schools of thought you may come across while researching education:

1. **Humanism:** Notable humanist figures include Carl Rogers and Abraham Maslow. Humanism in education emphasizes the need for genuine human connection, both student-teacher and peer-to-peer. This ideology, also called person-centered education, prioritizes empathy, understanding, and passion for academic subjects as well as personal growth.

2. **Behaviorism:** Using the work of B.F. Skinner and his research into operant conditioning, behaviorism uses Skinner's four consequence models (positive and negative reinforcement and punishment) to shape students' behavior in the classroom to foster learning. We look at the effects of behaviorism in the section Professional Issues during our discussion on zero tolerance policies.

3. **Connectionism:** This psychological model from Edward Thorndike was historically concerned with the connections between external stimuli or a student's environment and the activity or learning they are partaking in. Similar to behaviorism, connectionism links a consequence to an action, but in this case almost exclusively uses positive reinforcement to encourage actions. Many teachers use this approach when they aim to "catch their students doing something good," like having their materials ready for the lesson without being asked, and give specific praise for the behavior.

Democratic Ideals

Like in most democracies, education in America is heavily influenced by politics, and the government exercises power over educational institutions through the U.S. Department of Education, although most operational decisions are made at the school district level rather than federally. The current Education Department (ED) was formed in 1980 after President Carter signed the Department of Education Organization Act in 1979. The purpose of the act was to better support states and local boards in their daily operations and to increase the quality of and access to education throughout the country.

The ED is also responsible for overseeing federal bursaries and education loans for the estimated 11.5 million students receiving aid for post-secondary education. Outside of the question of governance, the cultural and democratic values of a country also impact how it approaches education and what it prioritizes. The United States has a few notable democratic initiatives in education which we will look at briefly here to give context to some of the issues we will explore later on.

In response to a growing demand for agriculture colleges in the mid-1800s, Representative Justin Smith Morrill of Vermont introduced a land-grant bill to fund one federally supported mechanical college in each state. Despite being passed by Congress, President Buchanan vetoed the bill in 1859. Morrill reworked the bill to stipulate that funded colleges would have to teach military tactics alongside trades like engineering and agriculture and brought it to Congress again in 1861. At the same time, the Civil War was ramping up and many southern states were seceding.

This made the act even more favorable because it was mostly southern states who opposed the bill and a new provision in the rewrite specified that states who seceded could not benefit from this program. In 1862, President Abraham Lincoln signed the Morrill Act into law. Within the same two months, Lincoln also signed bills to finance the transcontinental railroad and the Homestead Act to encourage people to settle in the west. This resulted in a new industrial boom for Americans and many of the colleges created by the Morrill Act, such as the State Agricultural College and Model Farm (now Iowa State University) and Kansas State University, are still around to this day and still receive grant funding so long as they maintain their originally mandated programs.

As education in America expanded, the philosophies and approaches varied so widely that it resulted in growing concern among educators about the future of American schools and students. As briefly mentioned earlier, by 1870, most states had made elementary school compulsory and they all provided free elementary education in larger cities. But there was a question about how to train young adults for their roles in society. High school was available, but attendance was not mandatory, and high school education practices were not as consistent as elementary.

Some schools thought memorization was the most effective, whereas others emphasized hands-on learning and the subjects offered by different schools had no consistency. In 1892, the Committee of Ten was formed to address this issue and come up with a list of suggestions for improving high school education. They held conferences and accepted reports from colleges and high schools across the country to address "the general subject of uniformity in school programs and in requirements for admission to college."

These conferences were incredibly in-depth, and delegates discussed issues ranging from pedagogical approaches to subjects and the topics covered therein (including the weight given to each topic and how long a teacher should reasonably spend on each), and how to approach students with different educational goals within the same classroom (should students going to college have different expectations than those expecting to go into the workforce). Finally, they looked at tests and what form they should take, as well as how they should be used to inform college admission decisions.

The committee's first recommendation was that children spend twelve years in school, eight in elementary (or grammar) school, and four in secondary school, though this was not expected to be mandatory at the time. Rather, the goal seemed to be for students to have a choice in when their education finished based on their life goals and family income.

In response to the question of whether students with different educational goals should be taught different things, the committee unanimously decided "that every subject which is taught at all in a secondary school should be taught in the same way and to the same extent to every pupil so long as he pursues it, no matter what the probable destination of the pupil may be, or at what point his education is to cease."

The committee conferences also came up with a proposed schedule for teaching certain subjects and determined that certain subjects like English, history, and mathematics should be taught every academic year in secondary school because of their correlation to students' performance in other subjects. The division of the sciences started at these conferences as well, as it was determined that physics and chemistry could be explored in more depth as their own disciplines in higher years.

A general consensus was reached that in order to best implement these recommendations, teachers needed even more training, and the Committee proposed that universities offer subject-specific teacher training courses so that educators could gain more insight into their subjects and how to teach them.

They, like Horace Mann, also emphasized that the disposition of the teacher was just as important as their training and maintained that teachers should be individuals who show strong moral character along with passion for their subject and for teaching. The result of the report and recommendations was a growing interest in secondary education, and the improved consistency led to higher quality outcomes.

The attitude toward education was shifting during the late 1800s and early 1900s, often called the Progressive Era, and secondary schools were gaining popularity as a place to learn skills—not just for college, but for life. This led to the high school movement that lasted from around 1910 until 1940. During these years, more students, particularly those of the middle class, decided to pursue secondary education.

Students of color are not included in this statistic, but we will look at the role race plays in education in a later chapter. The spike in enrollment also led to a dramatic increase in high school graduates, especially among women, and directly correlated with a noted increase in women in the workforce up to and during WWII, at which time enrollment dropped once again as teachers and students left to enlist.

NEA and NCLC

During this boom in high school popularity, the National Education Association (NEA), the same interest group who appointed the Committee of Ten, arranged the Commission of the Reorganization of Secondary Education. More people wanted the trades to be taught in high school and for there to be less focus on purely academic subjects. The Commission's report opens with references to the change in how factories were running, labor specialization, "and the breakdown of the apprentice system," which demonstrates their consideration for the changing political and industrial landscapes in their report.

The anti-child labor movement, for example, was growing thanks to the National Child Labor Committee (NCLC), a non-profit organization formed in 1904. The NCLC even successfully lobbied the government to create the United States Children's Bureau within the Department of Commerce and Labor in 1912, which was concerned solely with the welfare of children and their mothers.

Their research led to the Keating-Owen Act of 1916 which, while short-lived, put restrictions on the interstate sale of goods produced by factories which employed children under fourteen or mines which employed children under sixteen and various time restrictions. Even though the law was struck down nine months later after a Supreme Court challenge, by limiting the ways for manufacturers to sell their goods and materials when they used child labor, the NCLC and the Keating-Owen Act were a part of a growing sentiment on regulating labor conditions for children.

Cardinal Principles of Secondary Education

Child welfare played a big part in informing the Commission of the Reorganization of Secondary Education's report in 1918. They defined the Cardinal Principles of Secondary Education which specified the goals every high school should strive for.

1. **Health:** Health needs and education were to be included in every high school's mandate. Schools must consider physical health when planning lessons and lei-

sure activities and supply adequate equipment for such activities while keeping the school buildings and grounds clean and safe.

2. **Command of Fundamental Processes:** Teachers must balance theory and practice in all subjects, but in particular in skills considered fundamental, such as English and mathematics. Students should not be introduced to new and complex topics until they have mastered the previous ones, as per the curriculum requirements.

3. **Worthy Home Membership:** Boys and girls should be instructed in skills and ethics that make them valuable and contributing members to family life in adulthood. Social studies should consider an individual's relationship to the wider world, specifically their family and community in this case.

4. **Vocation:** Secondary schools should consider adding vocational programs to their course programming if their pupils would benefit from it (i.e. shop, farming, office). If the school cannot accommodate these additions, then they are encouraged to emphasize proper vocational etiquette, like teaching students how to appropriately interact with authority figures.

5. **Civic Education:** Students should be taught how to be considerate citizens and have a general understanding of national and international affairs. They should have a "many-sided interest in the welfare of [their communities], loyalty to the ideas of civic righteousness," knowledge of social institutions, and good judgment in interpersonal interactions and pursuits, among other things.

6. **Worthy Use of Leisure:** Leisure time should benefit the student's growth and personality development, and should be varied so that young people enter adulthood with a variety of interests that they can pick from to foster more specifically. Furthermore, the interplay between artistic, academic, and physical pursuits should be considered because love for one should not come at the expense of others.

7. **Ethical Character:** High school students must develop ethical character and it is up to the school to consider this goal in their programming. A spirit of service, personal responsibility, and initiative should "permeate the entire school," including the principals, teachers, and students.

The legacy of these principles lives on to this day as many high schools have some form of explicit character education in their mandates. Young people spend so much of their time in school it is generally understood that encouraging healthy development comes from a well-rounded education. Students should be provided with opportunities to grow in every way at school, not just academically. The next section looks at this moral growth aspect in more detail. It's hard to separate democratic ideals and politics from social influences because these forces impact education through a dynamic game of push and pull. It can often be difficult to tell which came first, the social movement or the legislation, and which had the greatest impact.

One would expect that the 1946 National School Lunch Act, for example, was enacted as a way to combat childhood hunger lingering from the effects of the economic depression in the 1930s, but it was more complicated than that. The details of the bill stemmed from a set of legislation that sought to offset losses farmers were facing from the market lull.

The original bill reimbursed schools for supplying meals for free or at a low cost to students when they purchased the food from local farmers in the subsidy program. Since then, the act has been amended considerably and is more focused on providing food for qualified students because a full stomach means better learning outcomes.

 Brown v. Board of Education

Perhaps the most divisive education decision of its time, the 1954 Supreme Court decision in Brown v. Board of Education resulted in racial segregation being declared unconstitutional. All public schools, elementary and secondary, had to desegregate or forfeit government funding.

The case started three years earlier in Kansas when the Topeka district school board refused to enroll the Browns' daughter at the school closest to their home because it was segregated. Instead, she, and other black children in the neighborhood, had to walk up to six blocks away to a bus stop from which they would be bussed to the nearest black elementary school one mile away.

While this doesn't seem like a great obstacle, some black children in other areas would have to be bussed over an hour away from home in order to get to school, and so many of the plaintiffs saw this as a battle for all minority children, not just their neighborhood. Linda Brown didn't even want to attend the closer school; her mother had attended the black elementary school herself and loved it. After a lengthy court battle and a lot of vitriol aimed at the Browns, including their eight-year-old daughter, the Supreme Court ruled unanimously that segregation was unconstitutional.

Prior to this, segregation was defended by a ruling referred to as "separate but equal" which claimed that segregated schools may have kept black and other minority students separate from white children but that the quality of education and opportunities resulting from it were the same. However, more studies and opinions were coming out showing that segregation had a terrible effect on the mental welfare of black children and contributed to systemic and inherent racism in white people. The Justices found that segregation was necessarily unequal and thus violated the Fourteenth Amendment.

The ramifications of Brown v. Board of Education were felt immediately. The decision ordered all public schools to desegregate but did not lay out methods for doing so or consequences for delaying or outright refusing. Many states and districts in the south did everything in their power to refuse desegregation and in one county, when finally ordered to begin desegregation in 1959, simply took the defunding option, which resulted in an entire school district being closed for five years.

Meanwhile, young Linda Brown started her first day at a newly desegregated school being screamed at, picketed, and degraded by white parents of current students. She went on to become an educator herself and spent her life fighting for the rights of people of color before she died in 2018 at the age of seventy-five.

 No Child Left Behind Act

The twenty-first-century has had its own share of controversial education legislation, most notably the No Child Left Behind Act (NCLB) which was signed into law in 2002 by President George W. Bush. NCLB had good intentions to "close the achievement gap with accountability, flexibility, and choice, so that no child is left behind" and passed with bipartisan support.

Provisions of the act stipulated that all schools receiving federal Title I funding must administer a standardized test to all students every year and that these tests must show Adequate Yearly Progress (AYP) in improving test scores. Schools that fail to meet the AYP for two or more years in a row are subject to remedial action, including being labeled "In Need of Improvement," having to develop a plan for improving education outcomes, and being forced to offer free tutoring and other support to struggling students.

On the fourth year of missing the AYP, the school is labeled as needing "Corrective Action" which could be as simple as school wide curriculum restructuring with training for teachers or replacing the entire staff outright. If this still doesn't result in change, a full restructure is planned in the fifth year and implemented in the sixth year which could mean turning it into a charter school (which we will look at later), hiring a private consultation firm, or having the state step in to run it.

States were responsible for setting their own AYP objectives, based on a set of criteria, so that each state's unique educational landscape was considered in the goals. States were also responsible for providing "highly qualified" teachers but could make their own definitions of what that looked like.

NCLB did a number of good things for public education, which is why it was so widely supported when it was first implemented. The first benefit was the added pressure on schools to identify and address achievement gaps through the use of standardized testing. It gave educators concrete data on where their students were struggling and as such allowed them to do targeted campaigns of improvement. If all of the math scores in a district were lower than the rest, for example, staff could target math education and look into why those scores were so low and provide relevant support to students. This in turn led to increased accountability for administrators and teachers. It meant that it would be harder for schools to cut corners because it would result in missing AYP objectives and bring the Education Department down on them.

NCLB also improved access to education for disenfranchised populations like those living in low socioeconomic (low SES) situations or students with identified learning disabilities, by allowing students with Individual Education Plans (IEPs) to use their accommodations on standardized tests and giving schools incentives for hiring teacher specialists. But NCLB has some flaws.

Many schools started using AYP targets and test scores to decide teacher salaries. This resulted in many teachers being forced to teach to the test, a method we cover more in our discussion on standardized testing in a later chapter. The short explanation is that teachers would feel pressured to sacrifice exploration and growth in order to make sure students knew how to do well on a standardized test so that they could protect their employment.

Considering teachers have no control over who gets assigned to their classes, getting a group disproportionately representing at-risk or low achieving student populations could set a teacher up to lose out on a raise or job or even result in reprimand even when they did their best. Focus was put so much on bringing up the lower achieving students that gifted and high achieving students often got left out of planning and received less attention. NCLB fostered a mindset of focusing on the ones who would show the greatest improvement and leaving the others, gifted and otherwise, alone. NCLB was so financially driven that it ended up hurting many of the students it was supposed to help. Schools often cut arts and other extracurricular activities if they were at risk of not meeting their AYPs so they could funnel the money into academic supports, which creates new problems surrounding student wellbeing and mental health.

Overall, criticism of the act increased over the years as the problems presented themselves. In December of 2015, NCLB was replaced by the Every Student Succeeds Act (ESSA) under President Obama which changed many of the NCLB provisions but left the controversial standardized tests in place. ESSA gave much of the control and accountability back to the states and they can set more of their own objectives, with ED approval. However, in 2017, Secretary of Education Betsy DeVos suspended most of ESSA's changes and said that more consultation was needed before it would be implemented and used the Congressional Review Act with the Trump Administration's support to completely eliminate all federal accountability measures, leaving everything entirely up to the states. It's still too early to tell what the ramifications of this move will be.

Kindergarten

Throughout most of history leading to the industrial revolution, young children (mostly aged three to six) were seen as uncontrollable miniature adults who needed to be tamed by strict discipline and routine to get them ready for school and life. In Germany, however, more people were subscribing to the view that children were naturally curious and inherently good-natured and would be best served by primary education and socialization instead of harsh discipline.

The German educator Friedrich Froebel presented a series of lectures on the subject and described children as plants that needed the care of a teacher to help them grow and flourish. Hence, Froebel coined the term kindergarten, or garden of young children, to refer to primary education. Margarethe Schurz attended these lectures and remembered them when her family immigrated to the United States. When her daughter was three, she opened a German-language kindergarten in her home for her and her cousins but soon had to expand into a local building because other German families loved the idea so much and wanted Schurz to teach their toddlers as well.

Schurz met Elizabeth Peabody, an American teacher, who was also interested in the educational theories of Froebel. Peabody learned what she could from Schurz before visiting Germany to study Froebel's methods directly. When she returned, she opened her own kindergarten in 1860, the first English-language kindergarten in America. She championed the kindergarten cause and wrote several books about primary education and edited a journal called the *Kindergarten Messenger* which was published from 1873-1877.

The movement caught on quickly and in 1873 the first publicly supported kindergarten opened in St. Louis. By the 1880s, there were free kindergartens all across the country and primary school was an accepted part of children's education. Kindergarten was seen as an excellent daycare system for parents who could not afford childcare and allowed for women to find more work outside the home to supplement the family's income. It changed the general public's attitude toward toddlers and opinion of them softened, with many now agreeing that a well-socialized toddler who is given structure and discipline, balanced with the opportunity to play and nurture their curiosity, will be better adjusted as they grow.

 Single Salary Schedule

Most public sector jobs use the single salary schedule to pay their employees. In theory, it eliminates discrimination in salaries because it bases pay on two factors: years of experience and qualifications (degrees, education, success, etc.). It meant that schools could no longer pay elementary teachers less than high school teachers, women less than men, and minorities less than Caucasians simply because they were elementary teachers, women, or minorities. Single salary schedule was instituted for teachers in 1921, a time when not all teachers had a full university degree or post-secondary credits in their subject specialty.

That meant teachers were encouraged to get more education because it resulted in a higher pay while also benefitting their students. Some people refer to this salary method as merit-based pay and proponents say that it attracts stronger teachers and is a great way to move teachers to underserved areas. Single salary systems also allow for incentives like a base pay bump for working in a struggling urban school or rural areas experiencing teacher shortages. This system also does away with tenure and seniority, meaning it is easier to move or fire underperforming teachers and replace them with more qualified candidates. On the surface, merit-based pay seems to be the best way to attract high-quality educators, but it gets complicated.

The National Education Association is very outspoken in its criticisms of single salary schedules. The first issue is that standardized test results are one of the factors that go into teacher reports at salary review time. Standardized tests are notoriously bad at actually assessing student achievement as well as teacher effectiveness, so their inclusion is immediately questionable (see Tradition and Progress).

It can also foster a sense of competition between colleagues and put a lot of pressure on teachers to take courses they aren't passionate about just to have another qualification on their resume. NEA board member Bill Raabe says, "We must all be wary of any system that creates a climate where students are viewed as part of the pay equation, rather than young people who deserve a high-quality education…"

The discourse is ongoing and some cities, like Cincinnati, are experimenting with new pay schedules to respond to changing economic situations, social pressure, and new research on salary systems.

Social Rights Movement

The 1970s were the peak for the social rights movement as a whole, with many initiatives from the 1960s gaining momentum and even some federal response such as affirmative action and civil rights, gender equality, gay rights, among others. The 1970s were also a major time for antiwar protests, environmental activism, and personal liberation. Young adults were fighting for the right to self-expression and began pushing back against traditional gender roles and relationships, resulting in more LGBTQ visibility and the sexual revolution.

Many Americans had lost faith in the established systems of government, capitalism, and education and wanted radical change to fix them. This point of view is often called the counterculture. Many young people and progressives who were a part of the counterculture saw modern public schools as an example of how industrial capitalism and social conservatism had failed society. They founded and joined free schools, which were essentially educational communities outside the jurisdiction of the state.

Supporters of free schools were guided by the belief that learning should be spontaneous, organic, and otherwise free from a structure they viewed as too authoritarian and stifling. Like schools, free schools were funded by tuition and private donations, however they operated very differently. Free schools had no established curriculum, no grades, and no marking or tests.

This utopian fantasy hoped to create a new society founded on everything they saw lacking in the rest of American life. There was a lot of allure in the free school movement and people who joined often felt liberated and as though their actions could affect meaningful change in a chaotic world. However, their rebellious energy ran out and the movement faded during the early and mid-1970s and was all but gone by the end of the decade.

Religion in School

Prior to 1962, many states had laws requiring the Bible to be a component in public education, and schools often opened session with daily prayer. In the nineteenth century, the debate between Protestants and Catholics was at an all-time high and there were arguments over which version of the Bible should be read in schools. Most schools used the King James Protestant Bible, which had many Catholics concerned that their children would have a weaker connection to the church as a result. In Wisconsin, Roman Catholic parents actually took their district school board to court and the Wisconsin Supreme Court ruled in their favor, though not in the way they expected. While the ruling only applied in Wisconsin, the judges found that reading the Bible in schools was sectarian and as such illegally "united the functions of church and state."

The practice was officially banned in Wisconsin public schools as a result and the case is referred to as the Edgerton Bible Case. It took seventy years for this debate to reach the federal Supreme Court, largely due to a growing religious sentiment in response to communism. Communism expressly discouraged and disparaged all religious devotion.

The rise of communism in Soviet Russia from 1921-1950 saw religious persecution and some scholars estimate that fifteen million Christians were killed in prison camps at the height of the regime. With the majority of Americans being staunchly anti-communist at the time, it was a growing trend to devote oneself to faith to socially combat communist ideals. However, during the counterculture movement discussed above, there was sharp rise in atheism and agnosticism, which led to more opposition to school-sponsored prayer and Bible readings across the country.

When the Supreme Court heard Engel v. Vitale in 1962 and Abington School District v. Schempp in 1963, they made rulings that officially prohibited school-sponsored religious activity. The former case established that it was unlawful for states to mandate any form of prayer because it violates the Establishment Clause of the First Amendment. The latter case focused specifically on Bible reading and, when ruling that it was unconstitutional for the same reasons, one of the judges cited the Edgerton Bible Case as the precedent for their decision.

Despite a general consensus that schools should include an education on ethics and morality, there is no general consensus on what that looks like. Traditionally, given public education's roots in Christian schools and religion, morals were based on the Judeo-Christian framework and on largely conservative social ideologies. With the separation of church and state rulings resulting in most religious education happening at home or at worship, some parents are worried that public schools are lacking in moral and ethical education. We will look more at the religion versus secular school debate in a later chapter as opinions are still divided to this day (see Secular versus Religious).

 A Nation at Risk

With all of this social progress and counterculture influence, a lot of traditional conservatives were left feeling attacked and resentful of what they saw as entitled protestors demanding a neutral world give them special treatment. They formed what political scientists called the "silent majority" which sought to maintain "traditional" values and opposed progressive bills that ran counter to those views. One of the silent majority's biggest victories was electing, and subsequently re-electing, President Reagan, who was staunchly against the Department of Education and promised to, if not abolish it, defund it drastically. He created the National Commission on Excellence in Education which released a landmark report titled A *Nation at Risk: The Imperative for Educational Reform.*

One thing everyone from all political and religious stripes seemed to agree on was that America's school system was failing and needed to be radically reformed, the differences were in just how the system was failing. *A Nation at Risk* was the result of a group of eighteen people from various sectors (government, education, and private) reviewing a litany of research, surveys, and statistical trends from America as well as internationally. The report is divided into five categories: Content, Standards and Expectations, Time, Teaching, Leadership and Fiscal Support. In total, they made thirty-eight recommendations across these categories, some of which were:

Content: The Commission recommended that for high school, English be taught for four years; math, science, and social studies for three years each; and that elementary school students have education in a foreign language.
Standards and Expectations: They saw a disturbing trend of grade inflation (likely related to single salary schedules) and cautioned against using it too liberally, while also recommending that post-secondary institutions raise their admission standards.
Time: They "strongly" recommended that schools adopt seven-hour days with a two-hundred- to two-hundred-twenty-day school year.
Teaching: The recommendations were in line with previous reports emphasizing competitive salaries and high degrees of competence.
Leadership and Fiscal Support: The Commission encouraged the federal government to remember its valuable role in helping schools meet the needs of specialized student populations and that they must enforce compliance with "constitutional and civil rights."

The report set off a flurry of debate. An independent laboratory was unable to verify all of the report's data and couldn't replicate some of their results, and there were even rumors that the Deputy Secretary of Education was aware of the discrepancies and told the writers to "bury it." Other critics cited the fact that there was only one teacher in the commission and no educational expert (i.e. someone with their master's in education or child psychology) which didn't make sense for a report on education.

The organization Strong American Schools, released a report for the twenty-fifth anniversary of *A Nation at Risk* to see how impactful the commission had been and found that most of the recommendations had not been enacted or, if they had, not rigorously enforced because of "organized special interests and political inertia."

CONTEMPORARY ISSUES

Equity

Education has a history of inequality, including some gaps which are still apparent today. This is because improving access to quality education is not a question of equality at all, but one of equity, two terms which are often used interchangeably despite being very different in practice. Equality is when everyone receives the same treatment: the same lessons, materials, expectations, and supports. But not all students need the same things to succeed, this is why we have special education and gifted classes, IEPs, and 504s. Equity is when everyone receives the unique supports that they need to succeed, making education a "level playing field" for all. In this section we will look at some issues past and present that affect equitable access to education.

Perhaps the most common equity discussion is how to support students with special needs. Students with diagnosed learning difficulties or disabilities are entitled to an Individualized Education Program/Plan (IEP) and/or a 504 plan, each of which serves a different purpose and is supported by different legislation. These documents provide students with access to accommodations, which change how the child is expected to learn, and modifications, which change what the child is expected to learn. IEPs are required by the Individuals with Disabilities Education Act (IDEA), a federal law that guarantees free and personalized public education to children with disabilities.

To qualify for an IEP under IDEA, a child must have a disability that falls into one of thirteen categories: specific learning disability, other health impairment, autism spectrum disorder (ASD), emotional disturbance, speech or language impairment, visual impairment (including blindness), deafness, hearing impairment (other than complete deafness), deaf-blindness, orthopedic impairment, intellectual disability, traumatic brain injury, or multiple disabilities. IEPs are comprehensive legal documents that outline the plan for how, and what, a child with special needs will learn at school. This means that accommodations and modifications can be made to both the physical learning environment and the curriculum. IEP planning is heavily regulated and requires an IEP team consisting of the student's parents or guardians, at least one of their general programming teachers, one special education teacher, a specialist who can interpret evaluations from health professionals, and a district representative.

The entire team must attend all IEP meetings and work together to create a written document which includes annual education goals, the child's academic and functional performance, services they receive, accommodations and modifications for each of their classes, and whether they participate in standardized testing. States are eligible to receive additional funding for students on IEPs and can have it revoked, or face additional consequences, if they don't meet the requirements set out in a student's IEP.

A 504 plan is a little different from an IEP. They are regulated by Section 504 of the Rehabilitation Act of 1973, which aims to stop discrimination against people with disabilities. To qualify for a 504 plan, a student must have any disability that affects their ability to participate in general public education. Some students who do not qualify for an IEP might be able to get a 504 plan. Unlike IEPs, 504 plans focus on changing the learning environment for the student so they can learn in a general classroom.

This can be by giving extended time on tests or allowing tests to be taken in a different environment. It can also include accommodations like being provided a detailed outline of the course content at the beginning of the year and instructions for teachers to check in on the student more frequently. A 504 plan does not typically provide modifications to curriculum content or expectations like an IEP can. The requirements and process are also less rigorous than for IEPs, with no need for it to be a written document (though many schools do write them down) and the rules for plan team members are less specific. States do not receive extra funding for students on 504 plans but can still be held accountable if they fail to meet the needs of disabled students.

IEPs and 504 plans fall under the category special education, which is different from what we refer to as general education. General education means being in a traditional classroom with age-grade peers following the general curriculum plan. Previously, all special education students were removed from the general education stream and placed into a segregated special education classroom.

Included in IDEA is the Least Restrictive Environment (LRE) mandate which stipulates that students with disabilities be educated with their peers in a general education stream as much as possible. The intention is to reduce the amount of segregation of and stigma against disabled persons. Studies show that students with learning difficulties and disabilities do better when they are part of a typical classroom community and that, for most students, segregating them in a special education class does more harm than good. While integration is recommended by special education experts and researchers around the world, kinks do arise.

There are stories of children with special needs being locked in closets for time outs, being harassed (sometimes even physically abused) by their neurotypical peers, and being flat out ignored by their teachers. The problem, according to a number of special education advocates and researchers, is a lack of teacher training and a proper support network. One special education advocate, Hannah Grieco, summed it up in an article for Education Week: "Inclusion works when educators collaborate, get the support they need, and believe in the value of all students."

Numerous anecdotes and studies have shown that inclusion and integration can work and benefit not only disabled students but the rest of the students as well. According to some research, nearly 85% of students with exceptionalities can succeed in the general education stream with the right supports.

Furthermore, research has not been able to substantiate the claim that integration harms academic achievement for other students. In fact, there are social benefits to special needs integration because students learn how to be at ease around people with behavioral differences, fostering empathy and more positive relationships. Some districts struggle to fully implement special education integration because they lack the funding needed to put the proper supports in place, like educational assistants (EAs) or special education teachers who work one-on-one with disabled students. Overcoming these barriers through professional development and support from administration makes teachers better educators for students with disabilities and without.

Gifted Children

Another frequently underserved group in education is the gifted. The need for specialized education for gifted children was first advocated for officially by the American Association for the Study of the Gifted, established in 1946. The first support for parents and teachers was made available by the National Association for Gifted Children starting in 1954 but it wasn't until the Elementary and Secondary Education Act (ESEA) was passed in 1965 that the programming support was made part of federal law. From there, gifted education saw much development and in 1972, the Federal Office of Gifted and Talented (FOGT) was established to disseminate funds for gifted programs around the country.

The FOGT was actually closed for a number of years as one of many cuts made by the Reagan administration until it was re-established in 1988 with the Jacob K. Javits Gifted and Talented Students Education Act. The Javits Act sponsors research for identification of gifted students and best practices for their education while also providing funding to states to support gifted programs. Unlike IDEA and the Disabilities Education Act, the Javits Act does not guarantee that Congress will release the funding nor does it guarantee a right of access to gifted programming.

The federal government defines gifted students as "students, children, or youth who give evidence of high achievement capability in areas such as intellectual, creative, artistic, or leadership capacity, or in specific academic fields, and who need services and activities not ordinarily provided by the school in order to fully develop those capabilities." However, states are not required to follow this definition, though many are very similar.

According to the National Association for Gifted Children (NAGC), which conducts research under the Javits Act, a major misconception is that gifted students will do fine on their own in a general education classroom. NAGC compares this to allowing a talented athlete to train for the Olympics without a coach. Gifted students need additional resources and challenges in order to stay engaged with their education and develop their abilities.

Without these supports, studies have shown gifted students can develop behavioral issues, despondency, and even low achievement due to boredom and disinterest. Gifted programming is also often perceived as elitist. Gifted programs are not meant to imply that students are better than the rest of their schoolmates, gifted is simply an identifier like diagnoses for students with disabilities, meant to get them the support they need. Secondly, this myth of elitism is also the result of systemic discrimination and flaws.

Gifted programs were, and sometimes still are, most easily available to white, and to a lesser degree Asian, middle- to upper-class students in districts where the schools and parents can afford assessment and placement in gifted programming. In New York City, approximately 70% of the students enrolled in their gifted programs were either white or Asian, while only 23% are black or Latino. This is a complete reversal of their general enrollment demographics which are 70% black and Latino and 30% white and Asian.

Organizations like NAGC and others are advocating for changing not only the perception of gifted children and programming but also for a systemic change in the way we identify and place students. One way to do this is by making assessment a regular part of early education for every student, not just those whose parents pay for the testing. This would provide the opportunity for every gifted student to be identified regardless of their race or socioeconomic status. Another idea gaining traction is that schools should transition to providing more individualized curriculum to every student, not just those with IEPs or gifted labels. As we will see in our later discussion on curriculum (see Curriculum), research is showing more that personalized learning can improve achievement outcomes and that inclusive practices like differentiation benefit the whole class.

 Title IX

During the debate over the Civil Rights Act of 1962, Senator Barry Goldwater said that morality could not be legislated. In response, Martin Luther King Jr. said, "Morality cannot be legislated, but behavior can be regulated. Judicial decrees may not change the heart, but they can restrain the heartless." Access to quality education is a right for all under federal legislation and there are a number of laws and amendments specifically written to address inequality in education for people of color, women, and members of the LGBTQ+ community. While states vary widely in the extent and wording of their anti-discrimination legislation, there are two main federal laws protecting students from being ill-treated at or excluded from public schools.

The first is Title IX of the Education Amendments of 1972 which states that "[n]o person in the United States shall, on the basis of sex, be excluded from participation in, be denied the benefits of, or be subjected to discrimination under any education program or activity receiving Federal financial assistance." Enforcement of Title IX is the responsibility of the DOE's Office for Civil Rights (OCR). The law applies to all schools, public and private, elementary through post-secondary, who receive federal funds. Private schools are included when any of their students are on federal assistance programs. Title IX's two biggest impacts have been in female athletics and university response to sexual harassment and assault.

Title IX has regularly garnered a lot of public attention and debate, most of which stems from disagreement over the intended definition of "sex." One side of the argument claims that sex also applies to gender and gender identity, which would mean that transgender and nonbinary individuals are also protected under Title IX. These were the guidelines established by the Obama administration amid growing concern over "bathroom bills" where transgender youth were being prohibited from using bathrooms and locker rooms that matched their gender identity. These guidelines were rolled back in 2017 by the Trump administration with the claim that it should be left up to the states to determine the legal definition and reach of "sex" in Title IX. As of this writing, this is still being challenged in the courts.

The second major piece of federal legislation affecting equity in schools is the Civil Rights Act of 1962. This act prohibits discrimination or segregation based on race, color, religion, sex, or national origin in voting and voter registration, schools, employment, federally assisted programs, and public accommodations (i.e. hotels). The OCR again enforces compliance with relevant civil rights laws in education including

Title IX and Title VI, which applies the Civil Rights Act directly to federally supported institutions like schools. In our look at colonial schools, we saw that girls were often excluded from comprehensive schooling and people of color were excluded entirely.

Other groups who did not qualify for public or parochial school were the disabled and, in some cases, children of immigrants, especially if they were not proficient in English. Though slavery had been abolished, people of color still faced discrimination in American society throughout the early and mid-twentieth century. In education, this was legally supported by a doctrine of "separate but equal," which claimed that even though black children had to go to separate schools, they were receiving equal education to their white peers. It wasn't until 1956 that segregation was successfully challenged by Brown v. Board of Education of Topeka (see Democratic Ideals) and outlawed.

The ruling did not affect change in every school overnight, however. Segregation of schools was not the only thing preventing people of color from getting a quality education. Residential security maps created when the National Housing Act of 1934 caused a boom in home ownership resulted in very clearly racially and class segregated neighborhoods that faced a lack of community services, unreliable transit, and increased crime. Because of carefully drawn school catchment areas, this also meant that the schools servicing these areas were going to be segregated because of the neighborhood's population. Part of the problem is the way property taxes work in school funding. Higher value neighborhoods have higher property taxes, which means the local school receives more funding. Better funded schools in turn attract wealthier residents and continue the cycle. The redlining done by the residential security maps caused so many neighborhoods with largely black and Hispanic populations to have such low values that their schools are poorly funded, which results in worse education outcomes and causes the feedback loop to work in reverse.

 Governance

In the United States, there are different levels of governance and each has their own responsibilities and limitations. On the one side, the benefits of having so many tiers in the system are that no one organization is overloaded and each is able to focus its resources more effectively, allowing for more customization. On the other, communication between so many tiers can result in bureaucratic backlog and delay important decisions creating more opportunities for disagreement as each stakeholder will have their own agenda. In this section we will look at each governance level, what they're responsible for, and some of the issues posed by the current system.

Department of Education

The highest level is the federal one, which is currently the United States Department of Education, typically abbreviated as the ED. The ED is led by the U.S. Secretary of Education and Deputy Secretary of Education who are appointed by the current sitting president. The ED is responsible for dispensing federal support to states, post-secondary grants and loans, creating policies for educational standards, and enforcing operational laws. The ED is not responsible for accrediting private schools and post-secondary institutions, nor are they involved in creating curricula. President Carter established a separate Department of Education to give education more attention and prioritize efficiency, allowing the government to better support state education departments, and create more accountability.

Opponents claimed that such a department would be encroaching on states' rights and, in fact, would be unconstitutional. Despite regular calls from some politicians to abolish the department over the years, the ED continues to operate. Most of the opposition seems to stem from a belief that the ED could violate the Constitution and other laws by dictating curricula and "control[ling] jobs," even though its current role in school governance does not grant it this power.

Daily operations, distributions of funds to individual schools, and programming decisions are made either at the state or local level. Supporters of the ED cite the need for consistency of care and support for vulnerable populations like gifted students and those with disabilities (see Equity).

State Board of Education

At the state level, education is managed by a state board of education, which is responsible for establishing and overseeing all of the public schools in the state. The state's governor carries all executive power but their powers with regard to education vary from state to state. It would take an entire book in itself to explore the different governance structures of each individual state, so for our purposes we will be focusing on what the typical structure looks like in general. Each state will appoint or elect a chief state school officer, whose title varies.

The chief officer leads the state department of education but cannot act without approval from the rest of the department officials who are appointed by the governor or hired by the chief officer. They are responsible for creating a yearly education budget, appropriating state and federal funds, developing curriculum standards, gathering information on student achievement, administering state-wide standardized tests, and generally ensuring that the department is operating according to relevant legislation. In some states, the chief officer is also responsible for setting teacher certification requirements and can issue, renew, or deny certifications. The chief officer is also typically the main line of communication between the department and the state legislature.

School Board

While the state governing body is largely responsible for managing the macro-level administrative tasks, the daily operations and curriculum decisions are left to the local districts. States are divided into districts overseen by a democratically elected governing body called a school board, board of trustees, board of education, or something similar, depending on the state. District borders and sizes depend on the population density of the area and sometimes follow city or county lines, while other times they encompass several smaller towns or municipalities.

In the cases of Hawaii, Puerto Rico, and DC, a single school board is responsible for all of the public schools in each area. The head of the district is called the superintendent and they usually have a deputy or assistant as well as a number of administrators. School boards are typically responsible for setting curriculum, hiring and assigning teachers and principals, coordinating professional development and policy information sessions, coordinating school maintenance and bus routes, and working with schools to collect data on student achievement to pass on to the state and federal bureaus. School boards also serve as the disciplinary body when employees or students engage in serious misconduct that doesn't constitute or falls alongside criminal activity.

School District

It is the local district's responsibility to create strategic plans to address achievement gaps, support vulnerable populations, and ensure the financial and administrative success of the schools they oversee. Local districts face a number of challenges to making effective policies and often get overwhelmed dealing with administrative tasks such as discipline and finance. This is further complicated by the bureaucratic network they operate in that can result in roadblocks and setbacks. Member turnover is also a concern when the new leadership has a different administrative vision and discards previous work done for a new policy.

Finally, the public has a huge impact on school board policies, especially when immediate action is demanded after a public controversy and the board members don't have time to research and debate a response. In the end, as Patrick McGuinn and Paul Manna outline in their 2013 book Rethinking Education: Governance for the 21st Century, a school board that struggles to identify its objectives and delegate efficiently will only struggle beneath the weight of school micromanagement and impulsive policies. Districts that empower and support their schools while adopting a proactive mindset will be more successful.

 Teachers' Union

The final aspect of governance that operates outside of the schools themselves is the teachers' union. Teachers' unions are organizations that work with their members primarily to resolve conflict between teachers and school districts by advocating for workers' rights. Using funds supplied by private donors and member dues, unions also often commission and publish education-related reports, host professional development conferences and lectures, and provide helpful resources to teachers.

Unions can represent teachers in the collective bargaining process, as well, but only in states where that is permitted. Most teachers' unions are affiliate members of either the National Education Association (NEA) or the American Federation of Teachers (AFT). You may remember that before the NEA was officially a union, they were already advocating for teachers' rights and the improvement of public education, having commissioned the Committee of Ten and other state-of-education reports. Unions in private schools are not included in this discussion because the regulations for private unions and teacher hiring are vastly different from the public sector. Firstly, private schools are typically allowed to hire non-licensed educators as teachers so long as they meet the school's individual requirements. Secondly, as a private institution they are subject to different union rules. If a new or aspiring teacher is looking to work in the private system and is curious about the union situation at a particular school, they are best served by contacting the school's recruiters directly.

Before teachers' unions were formed, it was an indisputable fact that teachers were being mistreated and underpaid by the system. The first issue was that most teachers were earning less than the average factory worker salary despite the extra education required to enter the profession. Secondly, working conditions were not enviable, with teachers often having to monitor cafeterias and hallways during lunchtime while not getting a lunch break of their own, and being required to help with school maintenance by removing snow or cleaning their own classroom.

Furthermore, school districts controlled teacher placement and could move a teacher without warning or consultation, potentially uprooting their entire family in the process. Unions fought for raises, better work environments, and accountability in the system and were instrumental in making the profession more appealing by reducing burnout and turnover rates.

That being said, research about union effects on the quality of education and learning outcomes is mixed. Some studies show a positive link between fully unionized states with collective bargaining rights and higher SAT scores but others have found correlation between high unionization and reduced graduation rates. One study even found that students in states with mandatory collective bargaining laws were, on average, slightly less likely to be employed and earned eight hundred dollars less per year as adults when compared to students in states without mandatory collective bargaining. The consensus seems to be that the students best served in highly unionized areas are the average achievers and that test scores tend to be higher, whereas the highest- and lowest- achieving students do worse overall.

Despite successful campaigns for higher wages and more teacher autonomy, student achievement only increased significantly in the worst-off school districts and remained fairly static in already average or better districts.

Union opposition to alternative school options is also a major criticism because many see it as impeding parent choice. Another choice unions complicate is whether to remove underperforming teachers. This is especially true in states with collective bargaining rights and tenure rules where unions, by default, side with the teachers unless gross negligence is proven.

Unions will fight for remediation and coaching and a gradual removal or transfer, rather than letting a school or district take immediate action. While this can prevent unwarranted and impulsive layoffs, it also hinders a number of legitimate terminations that can cause serious harm to student achievement. Still, it's hard to argue that every worker is entitled to due process when it comes to termination so this criticism is supported or opposed on a case-by-case basis.

Union opponents also criticize union political spending, saying that it gives them too much power and favoritism. When it comes to federal influence at least, the teachers' unions have actually been rather unsuccessful in lobbying for their preferred legislation. The Improving America's Schools Acts (IASA) under President Clinton was heavily criticized by the AFT, while the NEA wanted nothing to do with major reform at all. NCLB was given to unions and teacher groups for feedback before it was presented and all of the comments and suggested changes were ignored in the final version of the bill, leading to opposition from both union groups.

The NEA and AFT also struggled to work with state leadership to earn Race to the Top (RTT) grants and opposed waivers granted to states during the reauthorization of NCLB. Despite these failures at the federal level, unions continue to have this reputation of significant political power which some labor researchers attribute to a divisive discourse and poor public relations.

No matter a person's opinions on unions and union membership, studies show that unions are not the only issue facing public education. When looking at countries like Canada and Finland where nearly every teacher is a member of a union and their students regularly rank high on the Program for International Student Assessment (PISA), it's clear that unions are simply one piece of the public education puzzle.

Curriculum

The primary goal of every school is to educate its students, so determining what to teach is the number one concern outside of hiring competent staff. Even if the most skilled teacher is given the most intrinsically motivated students, if the curriculum is missing key elements and skills, then the school will have limited success. Curriculum can be defined as either a specified course of study, a collection of instructional goals, or the totality of a student's experience in an instructional program. In terms of education, all three of these definitions apply depending on the context. There are several subcategories of curricula (the plural of curriculum): explicit, implicit, excluded, and extracurricular. Explicit curriculum refers to the specific subjects to be taught and the knowledge students are expected to have by the end of the course (ex. English language arts, how to calculate the circumference of a circle).

The explicit curriculum is typically set by the state and is what students are tested on to make sure they are ready to progress to the next grade level. Also called hidden curriculum, implicit curriculum refers to the school culture and the skills or lessons learned through being in a structured social environment such as etiquette, morality, and teamwork and collaboration.

Many schools outline a set of missions and values which inform their hidden curriculum and many professional development initiatives encourage teachers to consider these skills and lessons in their planning. As one might expect, excluded curriculum are the topics intentionally left out of planning and in some cases are not allowed to be taught. This could simply be the result of limited time like in history class where it would be impossible to cover the expanse of American and world history in detail so topics are trimmed and divided into different grades.

However, excluded curriculum can also be controversial topics like sex education and creationism, where public sensibilities in an area clash with science and result in certain topics being taboo. Extracurricular refers to any school-based activity that doesn't take place in the classroom.

This means any sports, clubs, field trips, tutoring, and other such activities that help enrich students' lives and experiences. This discussion is by no means comprehensive, so those interested should use this section as a jumping off point for further inquiry.

 John Dewey and John Bobbitt

Historically, school curriculum was limited to basic reading, writing, math, and, in some cases, Christian morality. As with most educational theories, the idea of a formal curriculum came more into focus in the early twentieth century. This was thanks in particular to the work of John Dewey (see Philosophies, Theories, and Ideologies) and John Franklin Bobbitt. Bobbitt wrote the first textbook on curriculum called, rather simply, *The Curriculum*, in 1918.

He was not the first to write about curriculum and education theory, as Dewey published *The Child and the Curriculum* in 1902, though Dewey's work was more of a meditation on the conflicting views he saw emerging in the field. Bobbitt's book was "designed for teacher-training institutions as an introductory textbook in the theory of curriculum."

Both Dewey and Bobbitt insisted that learning was active and social and thus required a variety of techniques, specialized teacher training, and specified curricula that engaged students in their education.

However, unlike Dewey's more progressive and holistic approach, Bobbitt saw education far more pragmatically and said it should be directly related to job training and social expectations. He also decried coeducation, saying that boys and girls should be educated separately because their societal expectations were different. Bobbitt broke the process down into five steps:

1. Analysis of Human Experience
2. Analyze Current Job Market
3. Derive Objectives
4. Select Objectives
5. Planning in Detail

Bobbitt's method is very similar to how modern curriculum is developed. However, the job market is much more varied than it was in the 1920s, so analyzing the market for necessary skills is a bigger task (see Technology).

 ESSA

Part of the Every Student Succeeds Act's (ESSA) mandate was that all education and curriculum decisions be evidence-based. Unfortunately, while we have made a lot of progress in some areas of education research, curriculum is one where we actually haven't done enough studies to have strong evidence to pull from. Dr. David Steiner, director of the Johns Hopkins Institute for Education Policy and professor of education, writes in his 2017 report (Curriculum Research: What We Know and Where We Need to Go) summarizing the results of a review of K-12 curriculum choices, that "[w]e know very little about what makes a curriculum effective." What we do know is that curriculum is integral to successful schools, with a "comprehensive, content-rich curriculum" being a component shared by countries with records of high academic achievement.

Furthermore, there is such a thing as a strong curriculum, even if we have not created the taxonomy of features to define it. Dr. Steiner references the What Works Clearinghouse's (WWC) studies into what happens when you implement strong curricula and their findings that the Success for All reading curriculum improved student success by nineteen percentile-points compared to the one it replaced. Part of the difficulty in studying curriculum is that there is currently no standard definition of curriculum in schools or research.

As mentioned at the beginning of the section, context and speaker matter greatly when determining what is included when they say "curriculum." The field has a great need for a coherent taxonomy of curricula, or a classification system using a series of traits and components, so that researchers, curriculum writers, and education professionals can be sure they're measuring curricula using the same definition and standards.

What is clear from the Johns Hopkins report is that a carefully built and sequenced curriculum from a trusted source yields the positive results it does because it has been classroom-tested, modified, and "has been vetted by master teachers and coaches." Sometimes teachers and schools feel pressured to reinvent the wheel, as it were, due to social pressure from media and parents over the flaws in the current system.

They change what they are doing even in places where current methods are working in order to appease outside stakeholders and that ends up helping no one, least of all the students. What all of these reforms lacked, Dr. Steiner says, are evidence-based, content-rich curricula. What we're seeing in other countries, as well as to a smaller degree in the U.S., suggests that this is the area of focus if any reforms are going to be successful.

Common Core

Enter the Common Core Standards Initiative (CCSI or Common Core), an initiative that began in 2010 and is sponsored by the National Governors Association (NGA) and the Council of Chief State School Officers (CCSSO). The CCSI outlines the minimum standards of achievement for all K-12 students in the United States in English language arts and mathematics. They are meant to help K-12 schools better prepare students for postsecondary education and careers.

The Common Core Standards were developed by the NGA with support from the CCSSO. Development began with the goal of providing "a consistent, clear understanding of what students are expected to learn, so teachers and parents know what they need to do to help [students]" by creating standards that are "robust and relevant to the real world." The writers consulted with a number of professionals including teachers and researchers and also engaged in numerous rounds of extensive public feedback. They spoke with colleges and major employers to gain better understanding of what they were looking for in potential students and employees as well as what lagging skills were coming up in their screening processes. These are what Common Core sought to address.

Unlike most curricula, Common Core does not prescribe content or delivery methods (although it does have recommended topics and reading lists). Instead, it lists skills that each student should be able to perform by the end of a grade level. This is, after all, why they are called standards and not curriculum. But, as we discussed earlier, the semantics here can drastically alter discussion of Common Core's merit and legitimacy. A number of opponents to Common Core see it as breaking the law against setting a national curriculum, despite the fact that the U.S. Department of Education is not involved with the standards at all and that the CCSI is not mandatory for states to adopt.

Thirty-five states are currently using Common Core in their entirety, and four more states are currently reviewing their commitment to Common Core, possibly with the intention to repeal it. Several states who initially agreed to follow the CCSI have since repealed it and some have even introduced legislation to prevent it ever being implemented again. States were encouraged to adopt the standards in order to qualify for the Race to the Top grants established by the Obama administration. States could also qualify by writing their own rigorous base standards, though this didn't stop criticism against the move. In 2015, the ESSA added provisions to prohibit this kind of incentive in the future by preventing the Education Department from trying to "influence, incentivize, or coerce" states into adopting Common Core or any other standards initiative.

Some opponents say that the CCSI puts too much emphasis on standardized tests and, given that students are more likely to do poorly on them, the data on the effectiveness of Common Core are not reliable.

Some people support the idea of more aligned national standards but believe that Common Core missed the mark and there are other flaws inherent in the system. According to the NEA, almost 75% of their teacher members support Common Core implementation. The Trump administration has said it planned on abolishing Common Core entirely, but since Common Core isn't federally run, and the Education Department cannot force states to adopt or reject standards initiatives, there wasn't any movement on this. In the end, the CCSI is a voluntary program and just one approach to improving America's schools.

 Values Centered Curriculum

There is a not unremarkable segment of the education reform movement that supports implementing more explicit values-centered curriculum. Unfortunately, there exists no universal human code of ethics, values system, or moral framework. All of these concepts are subjective and inextricably linked to social context, which makes developing a means of moral education difficult.

According to some educational theorists, the focus should be on the moral reasoning process rather than the outcome. This means lessons could be more about building critical thinking skills, fostering empathy, and encouraging students to see a situation from every perspective before making a decision. By taking the presumed "correct" choice out of the equation, students are free to work within their own religious, social, spiritual, familial (etc.) moral framework while still engaging in the skills-building.

One common way to do this is to pose a moral dilemma to a class and use a variety of techniques to engage with it. A very popular one is called the Heinz Dilemma about a man who breaks into a medical laboratory to steal a drug to save his wife when the drug's inventor sets the price so high the man can't afford it and is indifferent to the wife's impending death.

This hypothetical situation can trigger serious debate and discussion in a classroom, with neither side being necessarily right or wrong. Teachers can use this problem as the basis for a formal debate which helps students practice the skills of oral presentation and using evidence to support a claim. But, is this values-centered curriculum or just an example of implicit curriculum?

Opponents suggest values are already inherently part of the experience of going to school. All schools have a code of conduct, rules and consequences, and expectations that their students will behave in a manner that maintains a welcoming learning environment.

Teachers and staff members are expected to model these standards as well. In this way, the school is already emphasizing and encouraging ethical behavior so there is no need to waste time and resources, making it an explicit part of learning for everyone. On the other hand, there are educators and parents who say that presenting students, particularly adolescents, with these kinds of dilemmas where there is no one correct answer helps prepare them for the kinds of situations they will encounter in the real world where the answers reside in moral, ethical, and legal gray areas. It also challenges students to consider their own opinions and values and to defend them in a courteous manner.

Social-Emotional Learning

Rather than teach values or morality, a number of experts advocate for social-emotional learning (SEL) which uses evidence-based practices to develop skills which correlate with strong emotional and moral reasoning. The Collaborative for Academic, Social, and Emotional Learning (CASEL) created a popular framework and curriculum for SEL that divides it into five core competencies: self-awareness, self-management, social awareness, relationship skills, and responsible decision-making.

Their programming is primarily targeted at elementary students, but studies have shown evidence-based SEL programs correlate strongly with reduced high school dropout rates, teen pregnancy, drug use, and mental health problems. This suggests that the discussion should focus less on the pragmatic definitions of values and right versus wrong and more on building student resiliency and reasoning.

Some people question the validity of SEL as a curriculum by asking how it would be measured or tested, but this argument is often dismissed as a non-sequitur, as skills can be considered beneficial and explicitly taught without having to be formally assessed. In the midst of this debate, some states, like Ohio, are considering implementing state-sponsored SEL programs in their schools as part of the ongoing struggle to improve education outcomes and help students become healthy and productive adults.

Underlying a lot of SEL and values-based curriculum is the idea of metacognition, a higher-order thinking skill defined as thinking about thinking or being aware of one's own cognitive processes. Metacognition also involves practicing regulating thoughts and cognition to achieve better results in all areas of life, though we are specifically looking at maximizing learning outcomes. According to the Canadian education resource network EduGAINS, metacognitive instruction:

- Helps develop a repertoire of thinking and learning skills
- Fosters confidence and independence in the classroom
- Encourages students to self-regulate their learning
- Enables students to self-assess the quality of their thinking
- Enhances responsible citizenship
- Increases awareness of learning styles
- Helps to decide which strategies to use in which learning situation
- Strengthens essential skills and employability skills

Metacognition

Metacognition must be taught explicitly for it to work properly because it relies on being able to dissect the learning process and assess how one's own mind is approaching a certain task. To do this, teachers first introduce the concept of metacognition and provide students with the vocabulary and steps necessary to analyze their learning and cognition. They can do this by taking learning styles quizzes such as Howard Gardner's popular Multiple Intelligences inventory, determining their predominant learning style, getting feedback from teachers, parents, coaches, and other trusted adults, and thinking about what it looks like when they notice they are learning.

Next, teachers should introduce a variety of strategies for skills like note taking, active listening, test taking, studying, goal setting, and project management. These should be taught when the situation arises for students to practice right away. Finally, giving students time before and after assessments and lessons to reflect on these strategies is important for reinforcing the skills while students are still practicing them. Over time, students will get better at self-regulating their learning and begin to prompt themselves to try something different or approach a task from a new perspective without teacher intervention.

Metacognitive education is not without its pitfalls, as a half-hearted approach implemented without proper training can result in reduced effectiveness at best and learned helplessness at worst. Learned helplessness, in the context of education, is when a student repeatedly does poorly on a task which causes them to believe that they are just incapable of performing it no matter how hard they try. In turn, this leads them to give up on the task altogether even when the situation changes and they have a chance to try something different.

It is most commonly seen in math classes where students will tell themselves they just aren't good with numbers and ignore opportunities to learn from another teacher or peer tutor with a different teaching style. Learned helplessness is associated with higher chances of depression and anxiety. Metacognition is a great tool for combating learned helplessness because it gives students more control over their learning and thus, they feel less like failures are happening to them as the result of outside, unchangeable forces.

Multiple Intelligences

When Howard Gardner was working as a psychology graduate student in the 1960s, he noticed a lack of arts in discussions on intelligence and wanted to expand the definition of human intelligence to account for talents beyond the intellectual. He identified eight major categories of intelligence, with a ninth one being more recently added to the list after more research, which he referred to as multiple intelligences. Everyone has some amount of intelligence in every category even though they may excel at one or more of them in particular.

1. **Spatial-visual:** The ability to easily visualize things and manipulate those mental images. People good at this can also often fill in gaps in the image or correctly visualize something they've never seen using context clues.
2. **Verbal-linguistic:** Language comes easily to this group and they are not only usually good at articulating themselves, but they tend to be very attentive and active listeners.
3. **Musical:** People with pitch, natural rhythm, and a talent for instruments will score high on musical intelligence.
4. **Bodily-kinesthetic:** This group tends to pick up physical skills quickly and have great control over their fine motor skills.
5. **Naturalistic:** This group tends to do well with animals and plants and pick up on the natural sciences quickly. They often feel most comfortable outdoors.
6. **Interpersonal:** Empathy comes naturally to this group and they tend to be quite social. They are typically good communicators and speakers and their peers enjoy their company.
7. **Intrapersonal:** This category represents knowledge of the self and self-awareness. While they are not necessarily introverted, people in this group are typically highly aware of their own strengths and weaknesses and know how to use that information in their lives.
8. **Logical-mathematical:** Puzzle lovers and logical thinkers tend to score high on this category. They are great at identifying patterns and usually do well on standardized tests.

9. **Existential:** This group is highly philosophical and have heightened awareness of the world around them, seeking to understand as much of it as possible.

Learning Styles

Educators especially tend to conflate these nine areas of intelligence with learning styles which are based on the personality type work of Carl Jung. Learning styles are the six main ways people learn, and using these categories can help both teachers and students. Teachers can plan their lessons around the dominant learning styles in their classroom and support their students effectively. Students who know which styles help them most can also advocate for themselves, especially in post-secondary school. Here are the six learning styles according to Brown University, which is the most commonly cited list:

1. **Visual Learning:** Using sight to gather information, especially with diagrams, videos, or written instructions.
2. **Group Learning:** Working with peers to complete a task, discuss an idea or topic, or participating in team-building activities.
3. **Kinesthetic Learning:** Using movement and touch to gather information, often doing well with active field trips, board games, or other manipulatives.
4. **Individual Learning:** Some learners prefer self-guided study and do well with solo projects and open-ended tasks where they can work through things by themselves.
5. **Tactile Learning:** Similar to kinesthetic learning, tactile learning focuses on activity. The main difference is that tactile learners especially like working with their hands.
6. **Auditory Learning:** Listening to lessons and instructions. These learners enjoy videos, lectures, podcasts, and songs.

Teachers should consider the diverse makeup of the learners in their classrooms and use tools like multiple intelligence inventories, learning styles, and even personality quizzes, to help their students practice metacognition. A teacher who uses these tools intentionally after making sure they themselves understand the methods and theories will provide their students with valuable skills that will last well beyond their education. Numerous studies have shown that metacognition and similar brain-based learning initiatives improve learning outcomes and modern education is responding to this research.

Scaffolding

Modern educators often structure curricula so that skills and knowledge build on top of previous learning experiences using a method called scaffolding. Much like the support structure it's named after, scaffolding is an approach to lesson planning that starts with teachers considering their students' prior knowledge and building units to help them reach the next level. The method relies on many of the principles of the zone of proximal development and the gradual release of responsibility. The term scaffolding was first coined by psychologist Jerome Bruner in 1976 during his work on the overlaps between cognitive psychology and education following in the footsteps of Vygotsky. By the 1980s, researchers and educators were trying to further codify scaffolding strategies and make them easy to implement. Arthur Applebee and Judith Langer from the University of Albany-SUNY identified five major features of scaffolding:

1. **Intentionality:** The task or lesson has a clear purpose or goal.
2. **Appropriateness:** The task or lesson is appropriately designed for the students engaging in it and their ZPD.
3. **Structure:** The task or lesson has been thoughtfully structured to follow a logical and natural sequence.
4. **Collaboration:** The teacher acknowledges student success and helps them expand their learning and does not focus heavily on their role as an evaluator.
5. **Internalization:** The teacher gradually removes guidance and support as the student masters the skill or knowledge and internalizes the information.

Further studies on scaffolding have shown that the technique is most effective when sufficient appropriate guidance is provided to the learner so that the ZPD is maintained throughout the exercise and that collaboration with peers and instructors is a major contributing factor in the success of scaffolding. Another critical factor is identifying and maintaining the optimal level of help.

This means knowing how to balance giving students hints, walking through an exercise with them step-by-step, or encouraging them to try again either alone or with help from peers. As teachers gain experience, they get better at identifying when a student has gone outside their ZPD and needs more support, a modified task, or is ready to move onto something more challenging. However, it can be very time consuming to plan a properly scaffolded lesson because it requires so many considerations to be made: student cognition, prior knowledge, chunking, learning goals, differentiation, and how to spiral back to topics students might miss or struggle with. Still, many teachers do their best to implement proven instructional strategies like scaffolding in their classrooms so they can provide their students with high quality education.

 Differentiated Instruction

The goal of every classroom teacher is to create an inclusive learning environment where all students can acquire or refine knowledge and skills. One common way to do this is by approaching planning using the philosophy of differentiated instruction (DI), often simply referred to as differentiation. This pedagogical approach involves planning for all learners by using multiple methods of content delivery and assessment. In order to effectively differentiate, teachers have to consider their diverse student community, the classroom environment, and the overall learning goals required for grade promotion or credit achievement.

There is a common adage in teaching that what's necessary for one is often good for all. This means a lot of common accommodations are actually beneficial for the whole class, even if only one student needs it. For example, most IEPs for students with ADHD suggest giving them a printout with notes from the lesson. Most other students would also benefit from having the notes at their desk, so it makes sense to provide everyone with a copy.

This also helps the student not feel singled out. The next things to consider are the major learning styles we looked at before. Teachers should incorporate as many of these as possible in their lesson delivery, so long as the method is appropriate for the content and learners. Learning to play basketball by individually researching the rules on the Internet is not very effective, after all.

Differentiation also involves looking at the learners as individual people and who they are outside of the classroom. Educators often call this "getting the students to buy in to the lesson." Students are more likely to buy in when they feel like the content is relevant to them, and it helps even more when they feel like the teacher knows and cares about them as a person. This can look like referencing the media students like in mathematical word problems or finding the sheet music to a popular song for music class.

Another important, but easily overlooked, factor to consider when examining a group of learners is their socioeconomic status. It may seem like no big deal to plan a large diorama as the culminating task for a book study, but some students don't have the funds or time to make something. If a teacher doesn't consider the socioeconomic status of their students and make the assessment equitable, they could end up ostracizing someone and harming their learning. The student may choose to not do the project at all because they can't afford it or feel like what they could afford would be embarrassing to present. The goal of DI is to remove barriers to learning, not create them, so teachers have to be aware of these issues. A good way to counter the socioeconomic problems of a diorama is to provide materials to the class to use and offer the option for them to bring in more if they'd like. Furthermore, there should be ample in-class time to work on this project, that way students who have to babysit younger siblings or work after school don't have to sacrifice schoolwork to other responsibilities. This way, everyone can complete the task, regardless of income restrictions.

Carnegie Unit

During the late nineteenth and early twentieth centuries, colleges, and universities started looking for a more reliable way to assess potential students. Previously, they used extensive testing but were finding it time consuming and unreliable at screening the best candidates.

Discussions led to Charles W. Eliot of Harvard University proposing a standard hour system for measuring student learning. The move toward an hour-based credit system at the secondary school level was endorsed by the NEA in 1894, but didn't see widespread use until 1906 when the Carnegie Foundation for the Advancement of Teaching was established and started enforcing one-hundred-twenty-hour credit standards in order for post-secondary professors to qualify for their pension program.

This became known as the Carnegie unit, a one-hundred-twenty-hour credit consisting of one-hour instructional blocks once a day, five days a week, typically over twenty-four weeks. Post-secondary institutions refer to this measure as a student or credit hour, rather than a Carnegie unit. This push toward standardization was part of a larger trend in education, as we've discussed with topics like curriculum content and teacher training, and was embraced quickly and enthusiastically.

For over a century, student contact hours have been a dominant force in determining whether American students achieve their diplomas. While it was initially a helpful tool pushing schools to pay closer attention to their academic standards, many experts are now worried about the limits it places on modern education. These doubts are even echoed by the Carnegie Foundation, whose president in 1993 notably said, "I am convinced the time has come once and for all to bury the old Carnegie unit."

He went on to call it "obsolete" and incompatible with modern education. According to a researcher with the Carnegie Foundation, the current credit hour system does not align with the intentions of the original unit and that it was not meant to suggest that "time equals learning, in the same way for all students." Given the variety of delivery methods and our improved understanding of student learning and pedagogical strategies, using instructional time with a teacher as the common denominator for credit achievement doesn't make sense. In 2013, the Carnegie Foundation started to explore new metrics with the intention of replacing the student hour altogether.

While most states remain partially or fully committed to the credit hour system, New Hampshire has done away with it state-wide in favor of demonstrating content mastery. Further complicating matters is the amount of state and federal legislation in which funding models specify "seat time" or credit hours in their wording, so moving away from the Carnegie unit is not necessarily a viable option unless legislation is changed simultaneously. Studies have shown with growing confidence that collaborative and flexible learning opportunities are needed in modern education, which will likely add fuel to the initiatives to abandon or supplement the Carnegie unit.

Professional Issues

A profession is a job that requires specialized education, has a comprehensive code of ethics specific to that occupation, is licensed, and is often overseen by a governing body that is responsible for regulating and advocating for members and enforcing the code of conduct. Teaching is one profession; others include, but are not limited to, doctors, lawyers, police officers, veterinarians, and trades like electricians and plumbers. While most jobs in food service, retail, and some office environments can be done with minimal on-the-job training, professions depend on employing highly trained individuals because every day is different and the job can change in an instant. According to some studies, teachers make 1,500 decisions during a six-hour school day.

That breaks down to four decisions a minute, and those micro-decisions are imperative for ensuring the safety of students, the success of a lesson, and the effectiveness of any classroom management strategy. These decisions get easier to make with training and experience so it's important that teachers receive adequate instruction in their duties. But teachers also have administrative responsibilities, outreach duties, and professional development expectations.

How effective a teacher is at keeping up with all of these responsibilities directly impacts their ability to make micro- and macro-decisions. This section is about some of the "behind the scenes" considerations and subjects teachers use to inform their decision making and lesson planning.

In order to become a teacher, the first step is to complete a bachelor's degree. Also called an undergraduate degree, a bachelor's degree is the standard four-year post-secondary qualification. When pursuing their degrees, it's important for aspiring teachers to think about what grades they want to teach. Some states require that elementary school teachers have post-secondary credits in math or science, which may be difficult if they are pursuing a Bachelor of Arts. With a bachelor's degree in hand, they can apply to a teacher preparation program. These programs range from one to two years and include courses on lesson planning, curriculum, classroom management, pedagogical theory, and supervised in-class practice.

While each state has different hour requirements, they all expect prospective teachers to log hours as a student teacher. From there, aspiring teachers need to pass the teaching exam for the state they want to work in. There are two companies offering teacher certification exams in America: the Education Testing Service (ETS) and Pearson Education. ETS offers the standardized Praxis tests while Pearson customizes tests for the states that commission them. Most teachers will take the Praxis route because it makes it easier to transfer certification once they pick a state to settle in.

From there, aspiring teachers will apply for certification with the state education department. Each state has different requirements and systems, but all will require passing a criminal record check. A lot of new teachers will work in their districts as supply teachers, filling in for day absences or long-term leaves, before they settle into a contract position at a single school.

During this time, it may also be necessary for teachers to obtain a master's degree, which can take anywhere from one to three years. Fortunately, many states also have teaching reciprocity agreements which allow for easy transfer of certification if someone wants to move. However, some states do require that teachers who transfer complete their unique certification requirements within the first few years of their move. Teachers looking to work at a private or charter school should check the school's individual requirements because some don't even require state certification or Praxis exams in order to be hired.

 Alfred Binet and Intelligence Testing

Alfred Binet, founder of the Binet Institute where Piaget worked while developing his Stage Theory, invented the Binet-Simon test, a hugely successful intelligence measure. His work had lasting impacts on the field and his tests were widely used. During this time, a German psychologist developed the famous intelligenzquotient, or IQ, measure we know today. However, it was Lewis Terman, a professor at Stanford University, who took Binet's original tests and revised them using IQ as the scoring method, creating the Stanford-Binet Intelligence Scales. This test enjoyed decades of success as the most popular IQ scale in the country. IQ tests have been used for military and police screening, college and private school admissions, developmental disorder identification, and more unscrupulous purposes such as justifying racial inequality and compulsory sterilization.

There are a lot of arguments against the administration of IQ tests that call into question their validity, reliability, and whether they should have any weight in legislative or educational decisions. The most committed detractors even put IQ tests into the category of pop psychology, which is a term with a rather negative connotation used to describe decidedly disproven or weak theories in psychology that get popular thanks to oversimplification, often in the name of self-help or wellness.

One main issue with IQ tests is the kind of intelligence they measure. Even Binet did not believe in the totality of IQ tests and acknowledged that they did not measure things such as creativity and emotional intelligence. They traditionally measure general knowledge and academic subjects, which does not provide a holistic picture of a person's success.

This leads into a significant IQ test drawback—labels. For a long time, IQ tests were used to identify people who were called "feebleminded" and used as proof for their exclusion from certain jobs or social interactions, internment in asylums and, in some cases, sterilization. Children who gain labels such as "slow" tend to believe they are not as capable as their peers and experience low motivation and self-esteem. On the other end, children labeled as gifted can develop unrealistic expectations of themselves, leading to anxiety or inflated ego which causes them to mistreat others. Studies show that effort and motivation are actually better predictors of success than innate ability, so labels can lead to stifling children who would have otherwise done very well with encouragement and grit.

However, these labels can also be helpful in getting vulnerable students the support they need. An IQ test is sometimes the first step in formally identifying a student with a learning disability or who is gifted. Furthermore, IQ tests are also designed to assess a variety of skills like working memory, logic, numeracy, and language proficiency. By breaking down a student's results into these categories, teachers can quickly identify lagging skills and respond accordingly. A student who struggles with language and communicating their ideas may still score high in spatial reasoning and numeracy.

When administering any IQ test or similar assessment, teachers and school administration should be aware of these advantages and drawbacks. They should also have a specific goal in mind for what they hope to learn from the data, whether it be to assess the effectiveness of a new teaching strategy or get an idea of their student population's strengths and weaknesses in general. As with any social science, we must be careful in discussing the significance and accuracy of psychological endeavors such as IQ tests. Our inability to adequately quantify human intelligence using current methods is by no means a reason to dismiss the idea altogether. Instead, we should use them carefully and acknowledge that they, like personality tests such as the infamous Myers-Briggs, have serious scientific flaws and their results are not immutable or infallible. They should be used along with a variety of methods to get a clearer, more comprehensive picture of student success and should be contextualized using professional judgment to inform pedagogical decisions.

 Standardized Testing

Another controversial method by which we measure student success is the standardized test. After NCLB was signed, the number of standardized tests skyrocketed, largely as a result of the new requirement for annual achievement testing. In fact, one study suggested that students will take approximately one hundred and twelve standardized tests if they are in school from kindergarten to grade twelve. W. James Popham, former president of the American Educational Research Association, defined standardized tests as "any test that's administered, scored, and interpreted in a standard, predetermined manner." This is why most questions on standardized tests are multiple-choice. They are either right or wrong and can be marked by machine to save time. Some tests have written questions, but there are strict rules for scoring to reduce the chance of biased results.

One benefit is that by having standard scales for assessment, the data from a standardized test is applicable to a number of uses. Firstly, the results can be used to compare the success of all students who take the test. This makes it easier to identify trends such as subjects or schools where students consistently struggle. Standardization often makes it harder for bias and subjectivity to impact grading as well. The data isn't just for assessing student success, either, as it provides a measure of accountability in the system. When a teacher's class does poorly on a test year after year, the data provided by the results allows the administration to determine the trend may be because of ineffective teaching methods rather than lack of student ability.

This can also be done school wide if a district notices that a school consistently underperforms compared to the rest of the area. This accountability is further enforced by the funding incentives in the ESSA. Teachers and schools which perform well on standardized tests can earn salary increases and bonus funding grants. While this may also incentivize cheating when reporting the results, several investigations into scoring anomalies over the years has determined that intentional misreporting happens quite rarely.

The other problem with standardized testing is the conflicted research on whether high-stakes standardized tests actually improve learning outcomes for students. While one 2011 literature review of the past hundred years found that 93% of studies saw improvement when using test-based incentives in education, more recent studies looking specifically at modern education dispute this claim.

The National Academy of Sciences (NAS) did a nine-year study during the first years of NCLB and found no evidence that testing has a consistent positive effect on student achievement and might actually be harmful in some cases. The biggest issue is that the tests are often discriminatory against English language learners (ELLs) and students with special needs. Due to the restrictions of standardized tests, many of these students do not receive the accommodations or modifications usually provided to them by their IEPs.

This makes the tests disproportionately more difficult for these already at-risk students. They also do not provide a comprehensive look at a student's range of capabilities. Standardized tests don't measure traits like creativity, reliability, leadership, curiosity, empathy, or resourcefulness, to name a few. Yet, most people would agree that these are just as important in ensuring a student becomes a responsible and functional adult. Students are also subjected to incredible stress during standardized tests, and some can handle the pressure better than others.

Test-taking and stress management skills are important for students to practice but the issue lies in the weight of the tests. Some students may do poorly on a test due to the pressure and the environment, but do incredibly well on an essay or project they have a week to complete. Which is the more valid assessment of a student's ability? Many teachers will say they're both important, but reducing students to standardized numbers that have such a major impact on their futures is questionable.

The NAS published another report on how standardized testing impacted teachers. By examining the Race to the Top grant initiative, the research council ended up cautioning against the use of test scores to assess teacher effectiveness because the link between the two had not yet been thoroughly demonstrated. More and more colleges are doing away with standardized testing as part of their application process as they realize that more holistic assessments provide a better idea of a student's potential, so perhaps this shift will result in similar changes in elementary and high schools, but that remains to be seen.

 *Professional Judgment*

A term used quite a bit in this section is "professional judgment." As a result of their training and experience, and with guidance from mentors and professional publications, teachers gain the ability to make appropriate judgment calls confidently. Teachers face a number of decisions every day, from the more typical like how much time to spend on a topic before moving on or what method they want to use to get the class' attention, to complicated judgment calls such as when to contact a student's parents or guardians or if they should reduce the marking weight of a test because a majority of the class did poorly on it.

Professional judgment in education is taking every piece of information you have about a situation, weighing the possible outcomes, and making the final decision with confidence while also being willing to admit if you make a mistake.

When regulations and laws don't cover a specific situation, professional judgment is important in order to make sure a student's best interest comes first. This is a teacher's legal duty, in fact, as they are in loco parentis while at school teaching. In loco parentis is Latin for "in place of a parent" and refers to a legal obligation certain individuals and organizations have when it is reasonable to expect that they act in the same way that a responsible parent would when making decisions for and regarding the child, so long as those decisions do not infringe on their civil liberties.

Initially, in loco parentis referred to disciplining students while in school and gave teachers the same rights that parents had in using corporal punishment when it was deemed reasonable. Since corporal punishment is no longer an acceptable method of discipline, modern interpretations of in loco parentis apply it to other forms of discipline. In loco parentis also gives the responsibility of student safety to teachers and other professionals in the classroom.

Teachers are to take steps to prevent harm coming to their students in cases where it is reasonably feasible. This is why many court rulings have consistently upheld that physical restraint of a student by a teacher (who has been trained to do so safely) is a reasonable action to take when that student is putting others in immediate danger. This is why it is so important for teachers to be adequately trained and receive support in developing their professional judgment. They are legally and morally responsible for the youth they teach, and they must be able to make those important decisions carefully and with confidence.

 Zero Tolerance Policies

Most conversations about professional judgment and discipline in schools eventually lead to discussions of zero tolerance policies, their purpose and intention, and their effectiveness. The first major zero tolerance policy in education came with the Gun-Free Schools Act of 1994, which required that every school receiving public funding suspend students for a year or more if they are caught with a weapon on school property.

On paper, zero tolerance policies are meant to deter unwanted behavior by imposing harsh penalties on students who break the rules regardless of context. The whole point of "zero" tolerance is that no leeway is given to students, even in cases where the transgression is unintentional or decidedly minor. Given the high number of school shootings and other acts of violence in America each year, it's understandable that administrators and policymakers would want to institute the most effective measures to keep their students safe. But do zero tolerance policies actually work?

Supporters of zero tolerance policies claim that they keep schools safer, reduce favoritism, and more accurately reflect the real world. They suggest that enforcing strict consequences for all infractions will cause students to think twice before breaking the rules out of fear of repercussions. Furthermore, by removing teacher and principal judgment from the disciplinary action, it is less likely that students will be treated unfairly due to favoritism. Finally, they believe that preparing students for life beyond school means exposing them to the same stakes as they will encounter in later life. A speeding ticket is the same whether you were rushing to the hospital or late for work.

However, there is no evidence that having a zero tolerance policy in place actually reduces student misconduct, favoritism, or better prepares students for adulthood. A 2014 study done by the Indiana Education Policy Center found that many school districts inaccurately reported on the success of their zero tolerance policies, or reported them without critical context and explanation of their research methods. In fact, between 1988 and 1999 (the height of zero tolerance implementation), only four credible studies on the effectiveness of school security measures were published.

In contrast, 165 credible studies were published in that same time period that looked at preventative measures like conflict resolution and classroom behavior management. Furthermore, the study noted that zero tolerance policies disproportionately affect minorities and already at-risk populations and these trends have been confirmed across twenty-five years of research into expulsions and suspensions. What all of this suggests is that more concrete research is done into zero tolerance policies and their effectiveness, and that this work is done by an independent body rather than the schools themselves to ensure accuracy and unbiased reporting.

Zero tolerance policies have resulted in a number of questionable punishments, many of them highly publicized in the media. In some cases, public outcry against the schools and boards resulted in the reversal or reduction of zero tolerance policies.

In 1999, an athlete at a school in Ohio was accused of using drugs but when they searched him, they only found a pocketknife with a broken tip. The student was a top golfer for the school's team and regularly used the tool to clean his golf cleats. He was charged with "possession of a dangerous weapon" and suspended for ninety days, resulting in him failing the semester. Also in 1999, a girl in grade ten in Florida was suspended for ten days after lending her friend a pair of nail clippers. The girl was a model student and wanted to become a doctor but now had a serious suspension on her academic record. The school even threatened expulsion, with the principal saying, "Life goes on. You learn from your mistakes. We are recommending expulsion."

These punitive measures typically have harmful effects on the students who receive them. Suspensions are among the strongest predictors for high school dropouts with a suspension increasing the likelihood that a student will dropout by anywhere from twenty-nine to thirty-two percent. That chance goes up almost ten percent for each additional suspension they receive. The problem with suspensions from zero tolerance policies is that they remove students from a structured and supervised environment, thus providing the opportunity for them to become involved in more nefarious activities.

Many of the students affected do not have a parent who can stay home with them during their suspension, so they end up being targets for the groups who recruit them. While it doesn't always happen, a student who is suspended is three times more likely to end up in the justice system. Despite all of the evidence against the effectiveness of zero tolerance policies, they continue to be enforced in many districts.

Technology Issues

The world looks very different than it did when the first colonial schools opened over a century ago. We have access to powerful computing tools by just reaching into our pockets, and can search a globe's worth of knowledge with the tap of a screen. Today's students have to be prepared to live in a twenty-first-century world and need skills and knowledge unique to this digital age. But there exist numerous barriers to digital learning, ranging from socioeconomic challenges to infrastructure deficits. Furthermore, ubiquitous access to technology is a privilege not provided to many of the world's developing nations where cell service is spotty and Wi-Fi access is a luxury. It may surprise many to learn that these problems can also be found in urban American cities. This section will explore what it looks like to live and teach in a digital world and some of the issues that come along with this new and constantly changing landscape.

Partnership for 21st Century Skills

Educators, employers, and government agencies have been increasingly interested in defining what success looks like in the twenty-first-century and how to prepare students for life in a digital society. As more industries transition to digital technologies and automation becomes more sophisticated, we've seen a decline in the skilled trades and factory work. Demand for programmers, computer engineers, and information and communication technologies specialists has increased considerably. In the service sector, there is more need for social media consultants and managers, web developers, and other positions related to e-commerce. These positions require specialized training and literacy skills, and education is shifting to respond to these needs. This has led to the identification of a list of important twenty-first-century skills. One of the major contributors in codifying the current list of twenty-first-century skills was the Partnership for 21st Century Skills (P21). P21 is a non-profit organization formed in 2002 as a collaboration between a number of key groups such as the NEA, the U.S. Department of Education, and a number of media and tech companies. Their efforts led to the development of P21's Framework for 21st Century Learning, which included skills and themes, as well as guides for how to implement the framework in classrooms. P21 divided their list of twenty-first-century skills into three main categories:

1. Learning and Innovation Skills – P21 refers to this category as the four Cs: critical thinking, communication, collaboration, and creativity
2. Digital Literacy Skills – skills involving understanding and interpreting new media and technology
3. Career and Life Skills – initiative and motivation, social and cross-cultural skills, flexibility and adaptability, productivity and accountability

Some skills, like critical thinking and flexibility, are not new to the information age, but new technology and situations challenge us to refine these skills to apply them to new scenarios. What P21 and other advocates emphasize is the need to think about what happens after technology enters the classroom. There is some opposition to teaching certain kinds of media literacy because it involves more screen time for students. Studies show, however, that students need to be taught digital media literacy skills and about the kinds of pitfalls and challenges they will encounter with these different technologies even though they already know how to use them.

This is where Henry Jenkins and his research team at MIT focused their efforts in 2006 with their paper Confronting the Challenges of a Participatory Culture: Media Education of the 21st Century. They looked at the kinds of social skills and cultural competencies needed to participate in modern society, especially with regard to the Internet and digital media as growing elements of participatory culture where individuals can easily create, consume, and interact with media culture.

They focused their research on four forms of participatory culture they called affiliations (membership and interaction with interest-based groups), expressions (producing media and products), collaborative problem-solving (such as alternative reality gaming, or Wikipedia), and circulations. According to Jenkins' team, "[a]ccess to this participatory culture functions as a new form of the hidden curriculum, shaping which youth will succeed and which will be left behind as they enter school and the workplace". How students today are taught to interpret and participate in the ever-expanding digital community will directly impact their success as adults.

Furthermore, Jenkins et al. outlined three concerns regarding digital literacy that counter the claim children and youth will obtain the skills on their own. Firstly, the digital divide, which results in unequal access to opportunities to develop these skills and knowledge. Second, there is a "transparency problem," when youth don't have the vocabulary or critical thinking skills to identify where media is shaping their perceptions of reality. Finally, there is what they call the "ethics challenge," wherein there is an "assump[tion] that children, on their own, can develop the ethical norms needed to cope with a complex and diverse social environment online."

There is mounting evidence that children and youth need formal digital media literacy training, and schools, where people spend most of their childhood, are the best equipped to provide this crucial education, but only if the right training and resources are put in place first.

 Digital Divide

The digital divide phenomenon is defined by Stanford University's "Plugged In" project as "the growing gap between the underprivileged members of society, especially the poor, rural, elderly, and handicapped portion of the population who do not have access to computers or the internet; and the wealthy, middle-class, and young Americans living in urban and suburban areas who have access."

Technology and the internet have become so ubiquitous in Western society that it can be easy to forget that living in America does not guarantee a person access to a smart phone or reliable Wi-Fi. The term "digital divide" originally referred simply to the binary having or not having access. Since then, the divide has continued to grow with the rapid evolution of digital technology and the definition of digital divide with it.

The first factor is household income and socioeconomic status. Unsurprisingly, when a person has to choose between rent, buying groceries, and paying their Internet bill, the Internet connection is usually the first cost they cut. This leaves them having to find free public Internet access at places like libraries where the connection is often slower and unsecure. In neighborhoods with high rates of poverty where fewer residents can afford Internet access, the issue is further compounded by insufficient infrastructure, meaning many households aren't even getting the speed or reliability they pay for. In 1999, one report noted that "the divide between the highest and lowest income groups grew 29%" and that families in the middle-class or higher (which is a household income of $75,000 or more per year) are twenty times more likely to have Internet at home than the lowest earners.

The U.S. Social Security Administration reported that, in 2018, approximately half of all working Americans were earning less than the median wage (around $32,838 per year). This means that while a family may not be in poverty if both adults are working, they are far less likely to have a home Internet connection. The NTIA report also found that race correlated with home Internet access, which has been corroborated by more recent Pew Research Center data showing people of color are less likely to be online. Given the number of other issues facing learners of color (see Equity), the digital divide can have a devastating compounding effect on these students.

The most direct way schools affect the divide is through homework assignments. A task force with the FCC found that approximately 70% of teachers assign homework that requires access to the Internet. Homework is already a contentious issue in many areas where students do poorly on assignments because they lack sufficient support at home. This is often because their parents or guardians are too busy or don't have the knowledge or skills to help. Students who have access to the Internet at home can overcome the lack of parental support and find the information they need online. Some may even be able to get online help from friends or their teacher. Students who don't have a computer at home and/or access to the Internet have considerable barriers between them and successfully completing an assignment.

According to a survey from the Hispanic Heritage Foundation, Family Online Safety Institute, and My College Options, 42% of students reported getting a lower grade on an assignment than they could have gotten had they had access to the Internet, and 50% were unable to complete the work at all.

The disconnect between the need for twenty-first-century skills education and access to the Internet is clear. Employers and researchers are saying that students need to be digitally literate to be successful in life, and yet there are many students who don't have access to the tools needed to practice these skills at home. The 2020 COVID-19 pandemic highlighted the digital divide when quarantines and social-distancing protocols put in place to stop the spread of the virus closed schools across the country. While many implemented online learning and home study, it quickly became clear just how many students relied on public Wi-Fi and schools to complete work as a number of families came out saying their children couldn't participate in remote learning.

Suddenly, the number of students at-risk of missing grade promotion or important credits skyrocketed. In New York City, officials combated this by working with internet providers to loan LTE-connected devices to students who needed them, but many were outdated and slow. Further highlighting just how important the Internet is to modern life, Internet service providers (ISPs) made a pledge to ensure that no one's Internet got disconnected during the quarantine measure, even if they were unable to pay their bills due to work disruption.

Schools and teachers need to consider how to reduce the weight of the digital divide at the local level. The easiest way to do this is with considerate planning. Teachers don't have to give out homework that requires the Internet, and by planning class time for research projects and the like, they can ensure everyone has the same basic access and ability to complete the work. If they have to assign homework, they should make sure students can take the materials home or assign reflections and opinion-based responses.

However, schools will run into a problem when there isn't enough funding for computers or devices. If every teacher in the school needs to take their class to the library or computer lab, the logistics of arranging that schedule would be quite difficult. Many teachers would have to compromise and change or push back assignments so that other classes could use the computers. Some schools don't even have a full classroom set of computers, so student access is further limited.

Funding initiatives are needed to give schools the resources they require to facilitate student success. In 2015, Qualcomm, with Samsung and AT&T, ran a program where they provided tablets with LTE capabilities to the sixth graders at a school in San Marcos, CA. Over half of those given tablets did not have wireless Internet access at home and were struggling to complete work as a result. Teachers at the school noticed an immediate change in the achievement gap and students reported feeling like they were better students now.

The Center for American Progress conducted research that showed if the achievement gap caused by the digital divide was closed, the U.S. economy would see growth of almost $2.3 trillion by 2050 when this generation of students is fully integrated into the workforce, which is quite the incentive.

 Technology in Learning

Debate over whether tablets and phones are learning tools or disruptions is ongoing because it is such a new challenge. The first iPhone, which drastically changed the smart phone industry and made the devices more attractive and accessible to the regular consumer, came out in 2007. Before that, it wasn't very often that school aged children would have cell phones of their own, and if they did, they couldn't connect to the Internet. Less than a decade later, the non-profit organization Common Sense Media found that 53% of children have a smart phone of their own by the age of eleven, and it jumps to 69% for twelve-year-olds.

It is now up to administrators and lawmakers who never had cell phones in class to make decisions for the next generation of students, and conflicting research and opinions make this a daunting task. In July of 2018, France passed a law banning all cell phone use in schools across the country for all students fifteen years old and younger, and similar bans have since come into effect in a number of places around the world.

One 2015 study from the London School of Economics monitored four schools and found that exam scores rose significantly after cell phones were banned and that low-achieving students saw the highest gains from the ban. Researchers at the University of Chicago published a paper in 2017 that demonstrated that even just having your phone off and face down next to you drastically reduces your cognitive ability. Even when participants thought they weren't being distracted by their phones, they did best on the cognitive tasks when their phones were removed from the room. There are also long-term cognitive effects from too much screen time with numerous studies showing that high amounts of screen time correlate with diagnoses of anxiety and depression.

The 2016 National Survey of Children's Health done by the Census Bureau found that children who spent seven or more hours in front of a screen a day (not counting school) were far more emotionally unstable, easily distracted, and even had difficulty making friends. This was compared to children who only had around one hour of screen time a day. Smart phones and social media use have also been linked with poor sleep among adolescents, which causes a number of physical and emotional issues including fatigue and melancholy. Finally, a Common Sense Media survey of middle and high school students found that 35% of students admitted to cheating during a test by texting, and 52% say they've cheated using the Internet.

However, a blanket cell phone ban makes it much more difficult to teach students the full range of twenty-first-century skills. Instead, the focus should be on teaching students how to self-regulate their phone use and make lessons engaging to help reduce temptation. One anecdotal report out of Stanford University said that smart phones and other devices have the power to dramatically improve student engagement and learning but "that the transformative effect on education depends not on the glorification of devices but on teacher support and a trusting student-teacher relationship. Another benefit is that using technology is that teachers are "speaking their students' language."

Digital communication comes with its own set of rules and ways of doing things, often called netiquette. Students today don't plan group assignments by sharing home phone numbers and arranging to meet up at someone's house. Instead, most will add each other on Instagram or Snapchat, create a group chat, and then someone will share a link to a Google Slides deck or Word Online doc.

When teachers use these same tools (minus Snapchat and Instagram to maintain professional boundaries), it's easier for students to integrate lessons and projects into their digital routine. Finally, phones can make a great organization tool. If a student struggles with paper organization, going digital might be the solution. Calendar apps have notifications which can help students stay on top of work by popping up while they're browsing TikTok to remind them something is due rather than it being out of sight and out of mind.

The key to using devices successfully lies in creating better habits and fostering a more productive relationship with our devices. Many students are so used to using their phones for recreation and socialization that breaking those habits is difficult, but not impossible. A major barrier to this shift is a lack of teacher proficiency and education on properly integrating devices into their classrooms.

Organizations like the International Society for Technology in Education (ISTE), Future Ready Schools, and the Foundation for Learning Equality host professional development workshops and provide resources to teachers looking to integrate technology into their practice more thoughtfully. More often we are seeing teachers provide lessons on finding trustworthy sources online, how to deal with cyberbullying, strategies for managing smart phone addiction, and netiquette for different social interactions which are directly related to Twenty-first-century skills. While some districts still enforce device bans, others are embracing technology and trying to find a way to work with it rather than against it.

 Remote Education

As we look to the future of modern education we have to consider the question of e-learning and what role remote education will play. The biggest appeal of e-learning is the ability to access the course anywhere at any time. If someone prefers to sleep in and finds they are most productive in the afternoon, they have the freedom to choose to work when they learn best. It also gives students and parents quick access to all of the course material at a glance, so if a teacher uploads slides from a lesson, students can review them as many times as they need to. Most online learning management systems (LMS) are also very customizable, allowing teachers to tailor them to their class' unique needs.

Common drawbacks of e-learning include a lack of routine and confusion around expectations and course material. Some students struggle with the lack of structure of online learning and are far more likely to fall behind. Studies show that reading digital content correlates with higher rates of distraction and reduced comprehension, but success in e-learning relies on being focused and self-driven. Furthermore, without direct access to a teacher to explain content in more detail or answer pertinent questions, students may also find that they struggle to grasp new concepts and stay motivated to learn.

Students who participate in e-learning also report feeling isolated from their peers and that the lack of a classroom community makes it harder to feel engaged. There is also a temptation to use more assessment methods that can be marked by a computer, since they're built right into the LMS. This means more knowledge-based assessments and fewer deep learning projects. You can't submit a diorama via online LMSs, so teachers have to find other, potentially less holistic, projects for students to demonstrate their learning.

A common model currently used by many schools is to combine in-class and e-learning models, where students are required to come to school but have access to a LMS for all of their classes. Teachers use these systems to post materials from lessons, copies of assignments and rubrics, and many also have forum sections where they can start discussion posts for students to reply to.

Currently, Michigan, Florida, Alabama, Virginia, and Arkansas all require that students complete at least one e-learning credit in high school and students who take e-learning courses report feeling more prepared for the independence required in post-secondary school. One study showed that students in grades eleven and twelve do better with e-learning than their younger peers and this discrepancy prompted the district examined to stop offering e-learning for grades nine and ten because they struggled so much.

This has been backed up by other research which suggests that, for now, e-learning should be reserved for when students have the maturity and self-regulation skills to succeed.

CONTEMPORARY AND PAST ISSUES

Tradition and Progress

Todd Rose, a professor at the Harvard Graduate School of Education, wrote in his book, "The hardest part of learning something new is not embracing new ideas, but letting go of old ones" (The End of Average). This text has spent a lot of time examining the ways in which education has changed over the last century and a bit, but there are a number of ways in which it's stayed the same. There is a constant push and pull between continuing to do what we always have because it seems to work and our current system is set up for it, and trying something new that research suggests might work better but requires some serious commitment to implementation and change. This is what Todd Rose is referring to in his statement above, this struggle to let go of old habits in the face of new knowledge, theories, and best practices. Let's look at some places in education where tradition and progress are butting heads over the future of the profession.

 Standardized Tests

Standardized tests are one tradition that we have come to rely on despite the mixed evidence surrounding their efficacy and proper use. Arlo Kempf, an expert on standardized testing and author of *The Pedagogy of Standardized Testing*, a book which examined testing in the U.S. and Canada, says that the problem isn't necessarily the tests but how we use them. He says that standardized tests are a tool like a ruler. Just like we wouldn't use a ruler to measure temperature or volume, we should make sure standardized tests are designed to measure what we want them to measure and not something else.

Students with dyslexia or dysgraphia (or English language learners), for example, may struggle with a word problem on a math test not because they are struggling with the math concept, but because they are struggling with the language. This question is now measuring their literacy rather than their numeracy. When looking at the results from the test, word problems and equations should be considered separately in terms of their relevance to student numeracy skills given the measurement discrepancy.

Other advocates agree with Kempf's assessment and say that without standardized tests, it would be next to impossible to accurately and quickly gauge whether a school or district is performing well or needs remedial intervention under the ESSA provisions. Besides unreliability of results, there are also consistent and troubling trends in results that show Hispanic and black students tend to score worse on the same test when compared to their white and Asian peers. While this is the result of a complex web of external factors such as school funding and systemic racism (see Equity), it could be argued that continuing to rely on standardized tests without first remedying the underlying inequity is actively, and knowingly, harming certain student populations.

Given that standardized tests like the SAT and ACT also contribute so heavily to college admissions, the question is what to replace them with. The National Center for Fair and Open Testing, or FairTest, proposes a shift to a three-factor system that reduces the weight and number of standardized tests, puts more emphasis on classroom-based evidence for learning, and a comprehensive school quality review (SQR) process. They recommend doing no more than three standardized tests before the end of high school, most likely one each in elementary, middle, and high school. This would put America's use of standardized tests more in line with other developed countries that have similar or better educational outcomes. These tests should also feature fewer multiple-choice questions and more long and short answer ones so students can demonstrate more comprehensive skills.

FairTest asserts that classroom evidence of learning assessed by teachers is where the focus should be when gathering data on student achievement. The reason for this is that the focus shifts from standardizing what the students do (the tests) to the criteria with which students are evaluated. Unfortunately, studies have shown that many teachers, especially new ones, have "limited assessment skills" so this new approach would need to be a holistic one that includes extra professional development and oversight. Teachers and students would both benefit from this approach because it would also require building more resource libraries that feature evidence-based and carefully crafted teaching materials for educators to choose from when they can't create their own.

What's more, research shows "that this process can be one with a degree of consistency more than sufficient for statewide comparability." All of this information would be gathered into an annual school report which would be made available to the public. Finally, the SQR, which is used in a number of other countries including England and New Zealand, is a comprehensive assessment done every four or five years by a team of skilled professionals. The team would spend several days collecting and reviewing information at the school such as student work, graduation rates, school-climate surveys, and would sit in on some classes as well as interview select students and faculty. After gathering information, they would write a report, discuss it with school officials, and then finalize and submit the report to the state as well as make it publicly available.

The final report would also include recommendations for ways to improve and highlight where the school was doing well. If a school is struggling, they will be assessed more frequently to ensure accountability for improvement. The picture of a school that is formed when all of the information from the three methods FairTest recommends is more reliable and comprehensive than the data from standardized tests. Currently, the ESSA still requires 95% participation in standardized testing with states left to decide what to do in cases where schools and districts don't meet the 95%. This requirement would have to be removed by the federal administration to make it easier for parents and schools to fully opt out of any of the tests.

Even some universities are experimenting with different admissions requirements, with some not administering entrance exams or considering SAT or ACT scores at all. While some started using alternative methods earlier, several schools were prompted to find ways to put less weight on test scores after the 2019 college admissions scandal (see Equity) called the reliability and validity of the tests further into question. Despite the numerous cheating and bribery scandals, the College Board (who administers the SAT) insists that "without an objective measure like the SAT, gaming the system to gain access to higher ed through wealth and connections would be much more common." They go on to claim that the SAT and ACT are also predictors of post-secondary school success.

The research that demonstrates this correlation is questionable, however, because the College Board is the primary sponsor for the study, and it contradicts numerous other studies that show the best predictor of college achievement is a student's performance in high school. Furthermore, one three-year-long study of colleges with test-optional admissions policies (students could apply with or without the SAT/ACT) found "trivial" differences in the success of students who submitted test results and those who didn't.

This finding was supported by another study in 2018, confirming that there were no impacts to overall school success rates. This study also found that schools with test-optional policies had increased diversity and representation among underserved. It would take a large group effort to truly change the way standardized testing is implemented in America, but the research is making such a change look more and more promising.

National Versus Local Control

In Governance, we looked at the interplay between the different levels of administrative control in education and some of the problems and benefits of having a multi-tiered system. With the most recent reauthorization, the ESSA considerably reduced the role of the federal government in education but failed to address the biggest concerns surrounding too much standardized testing and a continuing lack of school achievement score improvement.

As we saw, however, there are still a number of groups calling for the total elimination of the Department of Education and the shift of power more into the hands of states and local districts. Since we already looked into the arguments against keeping the ED, this section will focus on what an alternative governance structure could look like according to education researchers and experts. Unfortunately, complete local control, which is one such possibility, does not stand up to scientific muster. Research and models show the flexibility and customization offered by local control comes at the sacrifice of funding and quality education. It also provides little incentive to fix systemic inequalities facing many districts (see Equity). An independent study done by the think tank Bellwether Education Partners in 2017 found that despite the added flexibility for local and state control in the ESSA, apart from a few exceptions, "state ESSA plans [were] mostly uncreative, unambitious, unclear, or unfinished… It does not inspire confidence that states chose not to submit plans that advanced educational opportunities in bold and innovative ways…"

Even Betsy DeVos, Education Secretary for the Trump administration and long-time local control advocate, said of the current plans, "ESSA was enacted partially in response to the widespread calls from state school chiefs to give you the flexibility and opportunity to address your state's unique challenges... Well, this law gives you that chance. The trouble is, I don't see much evidence that you've yet seized it."

The Bellwether report reminded readers that the ESSA outlines only minimum requirements and does not prohibit states from aiming higher than the recommended standards or experimenting with new ideas and practices. Yet there remains a general preference for maintaining the status quo. There is a thought among many experts that a lot of this has to do with the incoherent governance structure putting too much emphasis on bureaucracy.

The current system as a whole does not incentivize adventurous and bold policies. Perhaps surprisingly, the idea of a multi-tiered system isn't necessarily a bad one, especially in a country as large and diverse as the United States. So long as every level of governance has a clear purpose and there is less overlap of responsibilities across levels, each of the federal, state, and local offices have a role to play in improving education outcomes.

Education Policy

If you ask many experts like Jack Jennings, former president of the Center on Education Policy who has served as a general counsel for the U.S. House of Representatives' Committee on Education and Labor, the problem is not the fact that there is federal involvement in education but the form it takes. The current ESSA "rests on the same faulty foundation as NCLB: ...that pressuring teachers and administrators to raise test scores will lead to better instruction... After 15 years of this sort of test-driven reform, there is no solid evidence to suggest that this strategy works."

Jennings outlines the role the federal government has played in education where it was absolutely necessary for them to step in, and many of these instances were directly related to civil rights, such as establishing schools for freed slaves when the Southern states refused to educate them, or national initiatives, like sponsoring efforts to increase STEM education to win the Space Race. He remarks, "When local leaders are unable or unwilling to provide for all children's needs, federal policymakers have an obligation to become involved." They should limit this involvement to providing more robust funding, sponsoring better teacher education and recruitment, and providing better incentives and accountability for states to improve.

Marc Tucker, an education policy and governance expert, in his report for the Center for American Progress, came to many of the same conclusions as Jennings and further proposed that control should be largely centralized at the state level. This would be similar to the systems in place in Canada and New Zealand, two countries that are consistently rated among the highest for education outcomes. In Canada, the federal government is largely responsible for supplemental funding for public schools and creates policies for civil rights and access to education and little else.

The provinces write the curriculum and policies for the province, dispense funding, establish graduation requirements, and define their teacher education programs and standards. The local boards and schools are tasked with implementing the guidelines set down by the province while following the laws of the country. Tucker says that this is what makes these systems so successful: the clarity of who is responsible for what, or as he calls it, clarity of "where the buck stops" with regard to setting policy and standards.

This alignment does not exist in the current piecemeal system of governance where there is a lot of back and forth between the different levels on policy, accountability, and standards. Aligning the different levels through clear responsibilities and authority on different issues would not only reduce the waiting time between proposing and implementing new policies, but would also save money and time, allowing those resources to be spent more productively.

Tucker, Jennings, and others suggest that the future of American education is dependent on consolidating school governance with coherent roles and responsibilities. But, like any education reform, it will take a bold and unified effort to accomplish, and it relies on people being willing to forgo tradition and familiarity in favor of change and not an insignificant amount of chaos.

 Secular Versus Religious

The separation of church and state has long been a foundation of American governance which is why it is (more or less) against the law for public schools receiving public funding to endorse or sponsor practice of any religion. School sponsored prayer and other similar activities are considered to be a violation of the establishment clause of the First Amendment.

However, there is an ongoing debate over whether such enforced separation in schools is in itself a violation of the First Amendment right to free religious practice, especially in highly religious communities. Regardless, the courts have consistently upheld the idea that religion cannot be officially endorsed by public school programming. Instead, the schools are allowed to work with parents in their communities to make alternative arrangements if they request their child have access to more religious education.

Interestingly, while it has generally been considered against the First Amendment to use public funds to support religious activities, it is not actually a federal law. At the height of Protestant and Catholic conflict in the late nineteenth century, President Grant made a speech that declared church and state should be forever separate and actually suggested a constitutional amendment to that effect. Congressman James G. Blaine then made such a proposal which read as thus:

No State shall make any law respecting an establishment of religion, or prohibiting the free exercise thereof; and no money raised by taxation in any State for the support of public schools, or derived from any public fund therefor, nor any public lands devoted thereto, shall ever be under the control of any religious sect; nor shall any money so raised or lands so devoted be divided between religious sects or denominations.

The proposal became known as the Blaine Amendment and though it passed in the House, it did not succeed in the Senate and was never added to the Constitution. But its legacy lives on in many state constitutions where supporters of the Blaine Amendment successfully lobbied their state legislature to pass versions of the proposal, many of which are still in place today. The few remaining states, like Louisiana, simply defer to the establishment and free exercise clauses. By establishing and supporting legislation meant to keep schools secular, "the Supreme Court was assuring parents that public schools… would not compete with parents in their children's religious upbringing."

The Blaine Amendment has caused some conflict with grant and bursary programs where money can be earned by individual schools through applications. In one instance from 2017, the Supreme Court ruled that a Lutheran religious private school could receive funds from a state-sponsored playground resurfacing grant after Missouri had banned their application to the program. It wrote, "Denying a generally available benefit solely on account of religious identity imposes a penalty on the free exercise of religion."

The consequences of such legislation are being seen as harmful and discriminatory to many religious people, in particular Christian sects which make up the majority of religious practitioners in America. To answer some of their questions mentioned above, the PEW paper highlights several key cases in which the courts have ruled against religious expression. In Wallace v. Jaffree (1985), the Supreme Court overturned a law in Alabama which required public schools to include a moment of silence where students could choose to pray, meditate, or just daydream each day. Even though the schools were giving children the choice of how to use this time, the fact that one of the uses explicitly mentioned was prayer meant the Supreme Court interpreted this as school sponsored prayer.

One wonders what the outcome may have been for this case in the twenty-first century with our new understanding of how important mindfulness and quiet time is for people of all ages. Student-led prayer has also fallen to the Supreme Court, such as in 2000 when they ruled in Santa Fe Independent School District v. Doe that schools could not sponsor student-led prayer at their football games. In these cases, and in others, the main issue the Court had with the activities was that they were taking place as part of a larger event or initiative where other students were present and as such were being compelled to participate (even if that participation was simply watching it happen).

Widmar v. Vincent

The biggest decision with regard to clubs was Widmar v. Vincent (1981), which led to the Supreme Court ruling that schools could allow students to create religious clubs which operate on campus, but also made a later decision that, because schools are public spaces, no group could be prohibited from using the space because of their religious affiliation. A community group with Jewish affiliation, for example, could still rent the school after hours for an event even if that event would contain prayer. Congress even took a side in this debate after some schools pushed back against the Widmar ruling and created the Equal Access Act of 1984.

The act required that, in order to maintain access to federal funding, schools could not prohibit lawful access to their campuses on the basis of religion or political affiliation. The Supreme Court ruled that "no reasonable observer would see the school's recognition of a religious group as an official endorsement of the group's religious views." Public schools clearly have to walk a fine line regarding religion and clubs, but the rulings suggest that it's not impossible to balance the needs of a community with the legal requirements for separation.

Wisconsin v. Jonas Yoder

In another landmark case, Wisconsin v. Jonas Yoder, the Supreme Court ruled in favor of a group of Amish men who were fighting for official exemption from high school for their children. In the Amish tradition, higher education is viewed as unnecessary for their lifestyle as well as potentially threatening to their religious salvation. When three parents, one of whom was Yoder, had their children stop attending the local high school in New Glarus, they were taken to court for disobeying the Wisconsin Compulsory School Attendance Law.

In the County Court, they were each fined five dollars, but the Wisconsin Supreme Court overturned the conviction and ruled instead in Yoder's favor. The state, however, decided to appeal this ruling to the Supreme Court. Due to Amish beliefs against retribution, the trio of parents were not well equipped to defend themselves in a higher court.

A Lutheran minister, Reverend William C. Lindholm, stepped in and wanted to help with the case on the grounds of religious freedom and started the National Committee for Amish Religious Freedom. He hired legal counsel for the men as well. The Supreme Court held with the Wisconsin Supreme Court and agreed that states could not compel public school attendance where it contradicted with First Amendment rights to religious freedom.

They did stipulate, however, that there must be "evidence of true and objective religious practices" and that exemption cannot be granted on the basis of an individual stating a preference. This ruling is often cited in discussions over the right to establish and attend religious private schools and for homeschooling.

 Public Versus Private

Providing parents with a choice in how their children are educated has often been cited as a priority of the federal and state governments. While it's debatable to what degree they have been successful because of factors like accessibility and affordability, there are a number of alternatives to sending children to the local public school. We will briefly look at the four main options as well as some of the benefits and drawbacks to each option.

 Montessori School

First, there are Montessori schools, which are a unique kind of private school with a specific pedagogical ideology and practice to unify them. Montessori programs are also available in around five hundred public schools across the country. When the work of Italian physician Maria Montessori was first brought to the United States in the early 1900s, it was lauded by respected figures like Thomas Edison and Alexander Graham Bell.

Montessori developed a method of education which puts the child at the center and is based on the belief that children are inherently curious and wanting to learn. This applies to children with special needs as well, who Montessori spent a lot of her time observing and researching in preparing her method. The approach uses largely hands-on activities and puts a large emphasis on student choice. The American Montessori Society lists the following Five Core Components of Montessori Education:

1. **Montessori-Trained Teachers:** Teachers must be certified in Montessori pedagogy.
2. **The Multi-Age Classroom:** Classes have three-year age spans to encourage leadership.
3. **Montessori Materials:** Teachers use specially designed Montessori curriculum.
4. **Child-Directed Work:** Children have freedom to pick what to learn, fostering intrinsic motivation.
5. **Uninterrupted Work Periods:** Extended time when children get to work entirely at their own pace on the task of their choosing.

Montessori classrooms are also designed very differently from a traditional classroom in that they are divided into different zones or learning centers which are dedicated to different subject areas and activities. Furthermore, most Montessori programs use non-traditional assessment methods and grading systems that typically rely on anecdotal teacher assessment of student learning over time rather than letter grades and tests.

Despite the initial enthusiasm, the Montessori method largely disappeared in America, due in large part to a critique written by respected educator William Heard Kilpatrick in 1914, until the 1960s when it exploded in popularity. However, this popularity, coupled with a lack of a truly codified practice in the United States, has led to mixed results over the actual benefits of Montessori schools, which are further complicated by a lack of peer-reviewed research. A 2012 study compared the achievement results of students in three groups: one using almost exclusively Montessori-developed materials, one using less Montessori materials, and one in a traditional classroom without Montessori materials. What they found was that the highest achievement scores, as well as improved social skills, were correlated with a high use of Montessori materials.

So, while a school may claim to be Montessori, they are not necessarily following the principles to the letter and will thus result in similar outcomes to a public school. Unfortunately, the alleged benefits of a Montessori education are typically locked behind a high price tag. This means that parents not only have to find a high-fidelity Montessori school for the best results, but will have to pay for it themselves. This means it is often reserved for families of the upper and upper-middle class.

Private School

Private schools (other than those of the Montessori kind) come in a variety of forms and ideologies. The most common kind of private school in America is the religiously affiliated. Private schools have typically strict admission requirements and parents have to pay tuition for their children to attend. There are too many different kinds of private schools to look at, so we will instead look at some of the pros and cons of private schools in general.

The first downside to a private school is the tuition, especially because everyone is already paying for public schools with their taxes. Luckily, many states offer tax breaks for parents with children in private school, allowing them to get some of that money back. However, as many sources point out, tuition is nothing compared to the benefits of a specific kind of education, especially if that education is religious. A number of parents see the spiritual rewards of private religious education as justification enough for a higher price tag. Because of tuition, restricted acceptance, and school ideologies, the student population of private schools is also highly curated, which can be both a benefit and a drawback.

As we've seen in other chapters, studies consistently show that children exposed to a diverse social group are often more empathetic and socially well-adjusted than those in homogenous settings. Some private schools are more homogenous than others, so it is parent preference and beliefs that determine whether this is a pro or con for them. Strict limitations on admission mean that private schools can offer smaller class sizes than public schools, which experts tend to agree is better for student learning, mental health, and teacher productivity. Private schools also enjoy a large amount of independence from federal and state regulation, which means they have more control over their daily operations and curricula.

This can easily become a problem, though, if the school is led by an administration who doesn't have students' best interests in mind or engage in unscientifically tested practices. Where private schools fall behind is often in programming for children with special needs. Unless the school is specifically designed to cater to the needs of children with learning and developmental disabilities, the private system is usually not a good choice for their parents. Students with special needs are legally protected in the public system, but since private schools choose their students, they could easily deny admission to children with disabilities. Not all will, however, and there are schools willing to work with parents to make sure their child receives a full and appropriate education.

Unfortunately for private schools, a recent study of more than one thousand students found that when socio-demographic factors are controlled for (which means any correlation they contribute to is removed or adjusted as close to neutral as possible), the academic benefits of private education disappeared. Even low-income students enrolled in private schools had only marginal increases in academic achievement compared to public school.

This study is part of a growing initiative to re-examine old literature suggesting private school is superior to public school and ensure that their results can be replicated when controlling for factors we now know heavily contribute to student success that have nothing to do with the school or curriculum (i.e. parents' level of education, family income). With the Trump administration's desire to increase charter school options and expand voucher programs to make private education more available, studies like this one call the move into question.

On the whole, public schools may have their flaws, some more than others, but are actually on par with most private and charter school options. Until more research is done and all of the factors examined, it is up to parents to use the resources available to them to make the educational decisions they feel are right for their children.

 Charter Schools

In between the public and private systems are the charter schools, which are publicly funded on a per pupil basis, though many also received private donations, and are independently run. A charter school is established through a contract with either the state or local district school board, depending on the legislation. The contract outlines the performance standards the school has to meet in order to maintain funding and autonomy. Charter agreements allow for flexibility in curriculum and delivery methods and provide more options for parents, especially if their child is looking for a specialty program like a performing or fine arts intensive or in-depth STEM education. They are required to follow any state curriculum regulations, even though they have flexibility in emphasis and delivery. While many charter schools have an application process, they often function more like an interview where the parents with their potential student and the school all get to know each other to determine if the fit is right.

Unlike private schools, however, charter schools cannot legally discriminate against students and cannot, for example, be an exclusive all-boys school. Since they are publicly funded, charter schools have to accept all applicants, though they are allowed to admit via lottery if they get more applications than they have seats for. Charter schools benefit from open admission, a flexible curriculum, and typically smaller class sizes.

Their semi-autonomous governance structure and freedom from certain regulations can be a drawback though, as they can choose to forgo things like state teacher certification and some even require parents to commit to volunteer hours. Charter schools are also not without their scandals, with one investigative report finding that charters in Ohio were four times more likely to misspend funds, and corruption and embezzlement are not uncommon. Furthermore, despite a well-intentioned shift in popularity to online-only charters to try and tackle twenty-first-century skills, virtual charters have been largely unsuccessful and have low performance standards and outcomes.

Vouchers

When parents want the opportunity to send their child somewhere other than a public school, they may qualify for a publicly funded voucher, which offsets or completely covers the costs associated with the new school. The rules for vouchers differ in each state, with some also allowing them to be used for homeschooling and some not offering them at all. Voucher programs are supported by advocates for parent choice and studies have shown they actually improve educational outcomes for the entire district.

One study out of Florida found that public schools who had to compete with local charters and private schools for students because of the availability vouchers tended to spend more money improving facilities and implementing programming than schools who didn't compete. Another study found that public schools in competition saw an increase in test scores. Opponents of voucher programs say that funneling funds away from public schools isn't an incentive to do better but is part of the problem.

Furthermore, other studies have shown that students on vouchers tend to do worse at private and charter schools than their non-voucher peers, which correlates with other studies we've talked about, which suggest socio-economic factors are better predictors of school achievement than the kind of school it is. Another debate occurs in states where vouchers are allowed to be applied to religious schools, thus funneling public funds into a religious institution. As of right now, the Supreme Court upholds the right of states to choose to grant vouchers for religious schools on the grounds that they are implemented equally to sectarian and religious schools and across different religions.

Education Secretary Betsy DeVos sponsored legislation in 2019 that would provide a five-billion-dollar tax credit fund to increase voucher programs, and has also called for states to allow them to be used for religious education to uphold the right for parents to choose schools that align with their family values, no matter their income. As of this writing, this legislation has not seen any movement in the House or Senate.

Civil Rights

On the subject of civil rights and education, we should briefly address the controversial idea of Affirmative Action. The original goal of affirmative action with regard to higher education was to address the systemic inequalities in education addressed above through countermeasures designed to increase diversity in colleges and universities. Though well-intentioned, the various guidelines and laws in the name of "affirmative action" have often been misinterpreted and misused or resulted in similarly racist and exclusionary practices against different groups.

Colleges began using race as a factor in acceptances in order to comply with anti-discrimination guidelines set out in the Civil Rights Act. Many of them had quotas, or a certain percentage of spots that were reserved for minority students to guarantee access for underprivileged applicants. This resulted in two things: diversity on college campuses went up and complaints about the practice being racist against white people. The first high profile challenge of affirmative action practices came in 1978 when Allan Bakke filed a lawsuit against the UC Davis Medical School after being rejected twice. He argued that he had better grades than some of the minority students who were accepted into the program and so the quota system was directly responsible for him not getting a spot he otherwise would have earned on merit.

The Supreme Court sided with Bakke and prohibited the use of minority quotas, but this did not end affirmative action. Schools were still required to guarantee a diverse population, so they began awarding additional merit points to minority applicants. This, too, was shot down by the Supreme Court in 2003 and they were told they could only consider race in acceptances if it was relevant to another factor. For example, if a student's CV mentioned that they were a member of their high school's all-black improv group, that could be given more weight when it came to their acceptance score because it implies diversity. Even this is currently being challenged with opponents saying that any metric that considers race violates the Fourteenth Amendment.

The general idea of affirmative action, however, has continued to be upheld by the Supreme Court and other District Courts despite admitting that there are still flaws in college admissions processes. There are a number of studies which have shed light on some downsides to affirmative action as well. In 2009, two researchers, Thomas J. Espenshade and Alexandria Walton Radford, released a book titled *No Longer Separate, Not Yet Equal* which analyzed some of these issues. Black students accepted into college programs are more likely to have been in the bottom 20% of their high school class compared to their white peers.

This also correlates with a higher dropout rate among these students because they are in programs they are not actually academically qualified for. This is referred to as mismatch as these students would have likely done well at a less competitive school. Studies also show that students are more likely to form social groups with people they are similar to in terms of academic strength and interest. So, when a student is mismatched, they are more likely to be friends with other mismatched (usually minority) students, causing further social segregation.

This reinforces negative stereotypes and can lead to a decline in self-confidence where the student now believes they are simply incapable of success. Mismatch has been shown to cause a number of problems, including a higher science and engineering dropout rate among black students and a disproportionate representation of black and Hispanic students in the bottom 20% of the class.

 ## Admission Preferences

It isn't just race that plays a role in college admissions preferences—a 2019 scandal involving several celebrities and high-profile executives showed that money is also a factor. After a lengthy investigation, the FBI laid a series of bribery, fraud, and money laundering charges against dozens of parents in a college admissions scandal like none before it. These parents engaged in a variety of fraudulent acts in order to guarantee their children spots in prestigious colleges.

Most of the accused, some now guilty, were celebrities including actresses Felicity Huffman and Lori Loughlin, and former Canadian Football League player David Sidoo. In some cases the parents bribed the schools using large financial "donations," in others the parents conspired with coaches at the desired school to forge an athletic history, and some even paid someone to take the entrance exams for their children. All of this was done through two organizations alleging to help students prepare for university exams and offer consultation on application packages: Key Worldwide Foundation, and the Edge College & Career Network.

Both of these were run by William Rick Singer and a number of conspirators. Singer cooperated with the investigation and helped build cases against his clients in exchange for lenience with a guilty plea. While the cases are still resolving in the courts, the scandal showed just how easy it was for wealthy parents to engage in disreputable practices involving the country's top schools. It has also led to a few senators planning to introduce legislation that would make donations to schools, where a person's child is attending or applying to, taxable to help discourage the practice, as well as find ways to curtail the artificial scarcity at the more prestigious colleges.

 ## Indian Child Welfare Act

There was another civil rights movement happening in the 1960s, though it was much quieter than women's suffrage, and the call for minority rights in large part due to systematic assimilation efforts by the government. Indian residential schools were common throughout the nineteenth and twentieth centuries, with the last of them closing as late as 1973. Supposedly, their purpose was to help "civilize" Native Americans and provide them with a "proper education."

In practice, however, residential schools proved to be abusive, and in many cases deadly. Children were typically forcibly removed from their homes, but sometimes parents were deliberately misled and let their children go willingly, thinking they would be allowed to return home for regular breaks and continue learning about their Native heritage. There are also documented cases of parents being bullied and bribed into letting their children go.

Once at the schools, Native children were forbidden from speaking their language and dressing in their traditional clothing, had their hair cut into typical Euro-American styles, and in many cases given new names. These actions led to a collective trauma for the Native American peoples with their culture being effectively erased. In 1891, attendance at residential schools was made mandatory for Native children and the government had the authority to withhold rations and money from families who did not comply.

Despite a report in 1928 calling for residential schools to teach traditional stories and languages as well as to allow younger children to stay closer to home, the practice continued well into the 1960s and early 1970s. Luckily, in 1978, thanks to a concerted effort by advocates, Congress passed the Indian Child Welfare Act which finally ended compulsory attendance. Now, Native Americans have the right to decide how their children are educated, whether it takes place on the reservation or off, and what language it's done in. Still, many generations of knowledge and culture have been irreparably damaged or lost entirely because of residential schools.

Multiculturalism

When schools embrace cultural and racial diversity, they are engaging in multiculturalism as opposed to creating a cultural melting pot. Traditionally, America subscribed to the melting pot ideal where people came to the United States to become an American, whatever their background was before. The idea was that these cultures (from mostly white nations like England, Germany, and Russia) could all come together and create a new, unique American identity, but one that wasn't monolithic or oppressive. Unfortunately, in practice, the melting pot led to many injustices including slavery, the Indian residential schools, Japanese internment camps, and others.

When a group wasn't seen as being "American enough," they were ostracized and harassed. More recently, there has been a movement to embrace an idea of multiculturalism instead where people can be American while still retaining the language, cultural practices, and pride of their heritage.

Schools are a great place to embrace multiculturalism because it gives students new perspectives and ideas to explore. Students learn about other countries and cultures and gain both empathy and knowledge as a result. Research shows that when students are exposed to a diverse group of peers, including people of different races and people with disabilities, their ability to think critically and engage in problem-solving goes up among other academic benefits.

 ## Sample Test Questions

1) How long will the average North American child spend in the education system?

   A) 1 – 12
   B) 11 – 14
   C) 5 – 15
   D) 9 – 11

The correct answer is B:) 11-14. It ranges depending on whether students attend kindergarten and the final two years of high school.

2) _____ were early colonial schoolhouses that grouped all students, regardless of age, in a single room with one teacher.

   A) Factory schools
   B) Cabin schools
   C) Common schools
   D) Open schools

The correct answer is C:) Common schools. The use of a common space in which all students were taught provided the name.

3) Which of the following statements regarding Horace Mann is untrue?

   A) Instituted and mandated "Normal Schools" for training public school teachers.
   B) Widely supported free public education in the U.S.
   C) Formulated the initial concept of multiple intelligences.
   D) Published one of the earliest American education journals.

The correct answer is C:) Formulated the initial concept of multiple intelligences. Howard Gardiner proposed the theory of multiple intelligences, not Horace Mann.

4) What is pedagogy?

   A) A debunked psychological fad that believed intelligence could be measured on the feet.
   B) Methods and strategies for teaching in academic settings.
   C) A research focus that emphasizes the importance of early childhood development in education and learning.
   D) A style of teaching that emphasizes hands-off instruction, and child-centered approaches.

The correct answer is B:) Methods and strategies for teaching in academic settings. This is typically drawing on research-based studies.

5) A child reacts with confusion when their father hides behind a door, believing him to have completely disappeared, and begins to cry. According to the Stage Theory of Cognitive Development, what stage would this child be in?

   A) Early latent stage
   B) Late preoperational stage
   C) Early sensorimotor stage
   D) Late concrete operational stage

The correct answer is C:) Early sensorimotor stage. In this stage, children lack object permanence.

6) A child observes their teacher pour two identical amounts of water into two differently shaped cups, one that is short and wide, and one that is narrow but tall. When asked which contains more water, they pick the tall glass. According to the Stage Theory of Cognitive Development, what stage has this child not yet reached?

   A) Stage of proximal development
   B) Preoperational stage
   C) Formal operational stage
   D) Concrete operational stage

The correct answer is D:) Concrete operational stage. Before reaching the concrete operational stage, children have difficulty understanding conservation, and so are more likely to make this style of error.

7) What stage of the Stage Theory of Cognitive Development did Vygotsky believe was the most susceptible to not being reached due to a lack of training and experience?

   A) Concrete operational stage
   B) Formal operational stage
   C) Sensorimotor stage
   D) None of the above

The correct answer is D:) None of the above. Vygotsky was not a proponent of the Stage Theory of Cognitive Development.

8) What are schemas?

   A) A method of teaching that relies on building upon knowledge the child already has to help them understand new concepts.
   B) A cognitive framework that helps categorize and identify concepts, experiences, and situations quickly.
   C) A process by which larger, more complex topics are broken down into smaller, easier to understand ideas for easier learning.
   D) A plan of instruction that outlines the goals of learning, and the expectations of the student by the end of the learning period.

The correct answer is B:) A cognitive framework that helps categorize and identify concepts, experiences, and situations quickly.

9) A child is learning to pronounce words in class. Through words like "tough," "rough," and "enough," they have formed a schema for the letters "ough" being pronounced as "uff." When they are told to pronounce "dough," they proudly reply, "Duff!" When they are corrected, they are forced to create a new schema for this new possible pronunciation. What has happened here?

   A) Adaptation
   B) Assimilation
   C) Accommodation
   D) Actualization

The correct answer is C:) Accommodation. The student has had to accommodate their schema as a result of conflicting information.

10) What did Lev Vygotsky subscribe to regarding the process of learning and development?

   A) Cognitive constructivism
   B) Behaviorism
   C) Social constructivism
   D) Pedogeological constructivism

The correct answer is C:) Social constructivism. Vygotsky believed that social situations played an indispensable part in development and learning.

11) What is the "Zone of Proximal Development" according to Vygotsky?

   A) The knowledge and skills a child has access to and can use unassisted.
   B) The skills and understandings that cannot be reached, even with assistance.
   C) Tasks that can be completed by the child, but only with the guidance of an adult or experienced peer.
   D) The social bubble that includes non-familial educators, such as teachers, counselors, and religious leaders.

The correct answer is C:) Tasks that can be completed by the child, but only with the guidance of an adult or experienced peer. The zone of proximal development was the area in which guidance would allow a child to accomplish a new task, according to Vygotsky.

12) Which of the following pedagogical concepts would John Dewey most likely support?

   A) The open classroom
   B) The factory school classroom
   C) Problem-based learning
   D) Informal education

The correct answer is C:) Problem-based learning. John Dewey believed that children's interest was a key factor in learning, and PBL attempts to use the teacher's knowledge to spark interest and foster attention in the student.

13) John Dewey subscribed to educational pragmatism. Which of the following describes his beliefs?

   A) School should be a place where students explore subjects independently in the way they want to.
   B) School should be a practical means to an end that balances job skills with intrapersonal growth.
   C) School should be used exclusively for vocational training.
   D) None of the above.

The correct answer is B:) School should be a practical means to an end that balances job skills with intrapersonal growth.

14) A class is given a standardized English language skills test, meant to assess their progress toward a specific degree of successful understanding and aptitude. This same test is given to all classes in the same grade range across the county. What model of schooling is being described here?

   A) The passive school model
   B) The open school model
   C) The standardized school model
   D) The factory school model

The correct answer is D:) The factory school model. This term is used to describe an education system that values standardized learning and tests for their efficiency in measuring achievement as well as their comparability.

15) According to Bloom's Taxonomy, which of the following is the most basic kind of knowledge acquisition?

   A) Creating
   B) Applying
   C) Understanding
   D) Remembering

The correct answer is D:) Remembering. Memorization does not equate to understanding and since even young children can memorize things, it is considered the lowest order of cognitive function in the learning taxonomy.

16) In Bloom's Taxonomy, what is the highest level of learning being utilized in the following situation?

A group of students is trying to create a popsicle stick bridge that can hold up a five-pound weight in science class. One student, recalling an earlier lesson discussing the strength of the dome shape of an egg, proposes the idea of using arches, and successfully argues that they should use them in their bridge.

    A) Remembering
    B) Applying
    C) Creating
    D) Evaluating

The correct answer is D:) Evaluating. Although many forms of knowledge and learning are used in any given situation, this student utilized evaluation to argue and support his idea to others.

17) What was the Committee of Ten?

    A) An organization created with the purpose of formalizing and improving high school education.
    B) A commission to support the integration of trade skills into high school education.
    C) A committee created to oppose integration and desegregation following Brown v. Board of Education.
    D) An initiative in 1912 to increase the number of mandatory years in education from eight to ten.

The correct answer is A:) An organization created with the purpose of formalizing and improving high school education. The Committee of Ten was a group founded in 1982 to address problems with the U.S. high school system.

18) Which of the following was not a recommendation of the Committee of Ten?

   A) Every subject should be taught the same way to every student
   B) Mathematics, English, and history should be mandated every academic year
   C) High schools should be a place where students can develop an ethical character
   D) Teachers should be offered specialized training as educators in subject-specific areas

The correct answer is C:) High schools should be a place where students can develop an ethical character. This was a recommendation of the Cardinal Principles of Secondary Education in 1918.

19) What was The Progressive Era with regard to American education?

   A) A period of increase in high school enrollment between 1910 and 1940
   B) A period of increased social rights progress beginning in the early 1960s
   C) A period of increased enrollment among women following WWII
   D) A period of increased adoption of new pedagogical measures beginning in the late 1970s

The correct answer is A:) A period of increase in high school enrollment between 1910 and 1940. As high schools began to be improved and attitudes toward them shifted, this era was defined by a substantial increase in high school enrollment overall.

20) Who commissioned the Committee of Ten and the Commission of the Reorganization of Secondary Education?

   A) The American Teachers Federation
   B) The U.S. Department of Education
   C) President Reagan
   D) The National Education Association

The correct answer is D:) The National Education Association. Before they were a major union, the NEA was a special interest group dedicated to improving public education.

21) Which of the following was not a recommendation of the Cardinal Principles of Secondary Education?

   A) Proposed development of "worthy" uses of leisure time among students.
   B) Create courses based on prevailing and predicted trends in the job market to prepare students for their careers.
   C) Use high schools as a means of preparing students to be considerate and informed citizens.
   D) Create courses to instruct students in being contributing members of their families and community.

The correct answer is B:) Create courses based on prevailing and predicted trends in the job market to prepare students for their careers. This was a view espoused by John Franklin Bobbitt in his 1918 book The Curriculum.

22) What was Brown v. Board of Education?

   A) A Supreme Court battle regarding the unconstitutional nature of segregation in education.
   B) A Supreme Court battle regarding the role and allowability of prayer and biblical study in public schools.
   C) A Supreme Court battle regarding the board of education's constitutionality in overpowering states' rights.
   D) An ongoing court battle regarding the acceptability of teaching creationism in science classes.

The correct answer is A:) A Supreme Court battle regarding the unconstitutional nature of segregation in education. Following this court case, schools across America were forced to desegregate or lose federal funding.

23) Under which doctrine was racial segregation in schools defended?

   A) Separate but equal
   B) Separate but the same
   C) Brown v. Board of Education
   D) None of the above

The correct answer is A:) Separate but equal. Defenders of segregation claimed that black schools were the same as white schools, just with a different population.

24) Which of the following was not a proposed measure of the early 2000's No Child Left Behind Act?

   A) Reduce the achievement gap among students within schools
   B) Enforce corrective action on schools that fail to improve learning outcomes
   C) Reduce the prominence of standardized tests, and provide teachers with more accommodations for individualized learning options
   D) Improve access to education for disenfranchised populations

The correct answer is C:) Reduce the prominence of standardized tests, and provide teachers with more accommodations for individualized learning options. The NCLA utilized standardized tests as one of its key measures of success, which is often a point of criticism against the bill.

25) Who was the first person to open an English-language kindergarten in the U.S.?

   A) Friedrich Froebel
   B) Elizabeth Peabody
   C) Margarethe Schurz
   D) Benjamin Bloom

The correct answer is B:) Elizabeth Peabody. After working with Schurz and Froebel, Elizabeth Peabody was the first to open an English-language kindergarten in the U.S.

26) A school opens that forgoes a traditional curriculum and class structure. Instead, students are allowed to explore their own interests, and allow their own personal desires to drive the learning process, with teachers providing assistance and guidance when needed, without formal grades or tests to measure achievement. What style of school would you describe this as?

   A) A common school
   B) A revolutionary school
   C) A free school
   D) A liberated school

The correct answer is C:) A free school. The free school movement was a short-lived idea emerging from the counterculture of the 1970s.

27) What popular movement in education resulted in more women entering the workforce?

   A) Bloom's taxonomy
   B) High school
   C) Scaffolding
   D) Open classrooms

The correct answer is B:) High school. When high school enrollment spiked during the Progressive Era, there was a corresponding spike in female graduates, leading to more women in the workforce.

28) What was one of the major issues regarding the Reagan administration's *A Nation at Risk: The Imperative for Educational Reform* report?

   A) Unreproducible results
   B) Unverifiable data
   C) Limited teacher/educator presence on the report's investigative board
   D) All of the above

The correct answer is D:) All of the above. Numerous issues have been discovered regarding the report, including unreliable results that haven't stood up to academic rigor since.

29) What act aimed at closing the achievement gap included a provision that established that schools use standardized tests to demonstrate Adequate Yearly Progress?

   A) The Elementary and Secondary Education Act
   B) The Every Student Succeeds Act
   C) The Javits Act
   D) No Child Left Behind

The correct answer is D:) No Child Left Behind. Schools that could not demonstrate they were making AYP were subject to remedial action, up to and including loss of funding under Title I.

30) What was the result of the Wisconsin court battle often referred to as the Edgerton Bible Case?

   A) Bible reading was banned because it illegally combined church and state.
   B) Bible reading was made mandatory in all Wisconsin schools.
   C) The King James Bible was banned from public schools, but not the Catholic one.
   D) None of the above.

The correct answer is A:) Bible reading was banned because it illegally combined church and state. The Edgerton Bible Case was then used as a precedent in later cases involving school sponsored religious activity.

31) In a classroom setting, all students have been provided with a written copy of in-class assignment instructions to refer to while they work, in addition to being told the instructions by their teacher. Additionally, one student with attention deficit disorder has been allotted extra time to complete the assignment, should they need it. In this example, the printout is an example of _____, while the extra time is an example of _____.

   A) Equity, equality
   B) 504, IEP
   C) Equality, equity
   D) Standardization, individualization

The correct answer is C:) Equality, equity. Equality provides the same treatment to everyone, while equity provides unique supports to those who need them.

32) Which of the following is true regarding both IEPs and 504 plans?

   A) Both allow for changes to be made in the learning environment and curriculum to assist students with disabilities.
   B) Both require the creation of a planning team including specific individuals.
   C) Both mandate that students be removed from general education environments into specialized classes.
   D) None of the above.

The correct answer is D:) None of the above. Only IEPs can guarantee curriculum accommodations, and 504 plans do not require specific people on planning teams like IEPs. Finally, steps have been made to limit the segregation of students in need of special education, meaning neither plan requires this action.

33) What do studies regarding the integration of students with disabilities into the general classroom environment often find?

   A) Increased attention toward individuals with IEPs leads to less attention to general students.
   B) Increase in abuse and/or harassment toward individuals with disabilities.
   C) Improvements in academic success for students with disabilities.
   D) Reductions in overall class performance.

The correct answer is C:) Improvements in academic success for students with disabilities. Studies often find that a majority of students with exceptionalities succeed in general education settings when provided with the right support and do better than when placed in segregated classrooms.

34) Which student population was the Javits Act of 1988 meant to assist?

   A) Students with disabilities
   B) Students from low socioeconomic backgrounds
   C) Students of color
   D) Students meeting the qualification of "gifted"

The correct answer is D:) Students meeting the qualification of "gifted." The Jacob K. Javits Gifted and Talented Students Education Act was the reestablishment of earlier programs aimed at identifying, investigating, and assisting gifted students.

35) The federal and state governments define gifted students as "students, children, or youth who give evidence of high achievement capability in areas such as intellectual, creative, artistic, or leadership capacity, or in specific academic fields, and who need services and activities not ordinarily provided by the school in order to fully develop those capabilities." What is untrue about this statement?

   A) The above statement is true.
   B) There is only a focus on intellectual and academic fields, not creative or artistic fields.
   C) State governments have their own definitions of gifted students.
   D) The federal definition also includes athletic achievement and skills as a potential gifted field.

The correct answer is C:) State governments have their own definitions of gifted students. Although state definitions are often similar, they are not required to utilize the federal government's definition for gifted students.

36) Title IX of the Education Amendments of 1972 prevents discrimination in education on the basis of:

   A) Sex
   B) Gender Identity
   C) Ability
   D) None of the above

The correct answer is A:) Sex. Title IX prohibits sex discrimination in any educational institution receiving public funds.

37) Why weren't schools desegregated immediately after the Brown v. Board of Education ruling?

   A) There were no penalties for not desegregating.
   B) The ruling was made during the summer while school was out.
   C) It was too much work.
   D) Systemic racism made it impossible to fully and truly desegregate.

The correct answer is D:) Systemic racism made it impossible to fully and truly desegregate. Redlining of predominately black and Hispanic neighborhoods made it nearly impossible for people of color to move out of their neighborhoods and no one wanted to move to a chronically underfunded school.

38) Which level of governance has the most influence over the daily operations of 3\ schools?

   A) The Federal Department of Education
   B) The State Department of Education
   C) The District Board of Education
   D) None of the above

The correct answer is C:) The District Board of Education. The federal and state departments affect more policy and funding while the local boards are responsible for more of the tasks that directly impact schools like bus routes and teacher placement.

39) Which of the following IS a power the Federal Department of Education has?

   A) Setting teacher certification requirements.
   B) Collecting education funding through taxes.
   C) Deciding school curriculum.
   D) None of the above.

The correct answer is B:) Collecting education funding through taxes. The federal government directs a percentage of tax revenue back to the states for education funding.

40) What are the two major teachers' unions?

   A) No Child Left Behind, Committee of Ten
   B) FOGT, IDEA
   C) National Teachers Alliance, American Teachers United
   D) National Education Association, American Federation of Teachers

The correct answer is D:) National Education Association, American Federation of Teachers.

41) "Private schools are required to hire state certified teachers." This statement is

   A) True, it is illegal to hire uncertified teachers in elementary and high school.
   B) False, private schools are allowed to hire whomever they want so long as they pass a criminal record check.
   C) True, because they receive federal funding from student grants.
   D) False, private schools don't have to listen to the federal government.

The correct answer is B:) False, private schools are allowed to hire whomever they want so long as they pass a criminal record check. Since private schools are not public entities, they are subject to different union and hiring laws and have much more freedom in staffing decisions.

42) A teacher in a state with collective bargaining rights laws has had consistently poor test scores and the district wants them removed instead of seeking remedial programs. What would the union do for this teacher?

   A) The union would step in and bargain for remedial programs first.
   B) The union would do nothing because it doesn't have to.
   C) The union would help the district remove the underperforming teacher.
   D) None of the above.

The correct answer is A:) The union would step in and bargain for remedial programs first. Unions in states with collective bargaining and tenure laws side with teachers by default unless gross negligence or criminality is proven.

43) A grade six class partners up with a grade two class for a Reading Buddies program. A few weeks later, one of the teachers notices some of the sixth graders inviting their reading buddies to join in a game of tag at recess. This is an example of

   A) Explicit curriculum
   B) Implicit curriculum
   C) Excluded curriculum
   D) Extracurricular activity

The correct answer is B:) Implicit curriculum. While the game itself is extracurricular, the action is an example of the sixth graders having learned respect for the younger children and the importance of including them in school life.

44) A group of students starts a lunch knitting club that meets in the school library. They get permission to advertise it during morning announcements. This is an example of

   A) Explicit curriculum
   B) Implicit curriculum
   C) Excluded curriculum
   D) Extracurricular activity

The correct answer is D:) Extracurricular activity. The students are engaging in a school sponsored activity, on school property, that isn't directly related to their classroom studies.

45) The Common Core Standards Initiative is

   A) A national curriculum sponsored by the U.S. Department of Education.
   B) A failed pedagogical strategy.
   C) A set of baseline skills and knowledge students should have by graduation.
   D) None of the above.

The correct answer is C:) A set of baseline skills and knowledge students should have by graduation. The CCSI is not government sponsored or created, nor is it considered a pedagogical strategy.

46) What is the problem with trying to implement a values-centered curriculum?

   A) Children are inherently amoral.
   B) Research says values-centered curricula don't work.
   C) There is no universal code of ethics or value system to base the content on.
   D) None of the above.

The correct answer is C:) There is no universal code of ethics or value system to base the content on. People with different religions, cultures, political affiliations, etc. all have different moral codes and values so it would be impossible to create a values-centered curriculum that everybody agreed on.

47) Social-emotional learning (SEL) programs have been shown to have what benefits for students?

   A) Reduced dropout rates.
   B) Less drug use.
   C) Better mental health.
   D) All of the above.

The correct answer is D:) All of the above. The evidence-based practices in SEL programs have been shown to have all of these benefits, among others.

48) What is metacognition?

   A) The cognitive process of thinking about thinking.
   B) The cognitive process of thinking about teaching.
   C) The pedagogical approach of chunking information.
   D) The pedagogical approach of sequencing content.

The correct answer is A:) The cognitive process of thinking about thinking. Metacognition translates to "above thinking" and refers to being aware of and regulating one's own cognitive processes.

49) Which of the following is NOT one of Howard Gardner's identified multiple intelligences?

   A) Spatial-visual
   B) Naturalistic
   C) International
   D) Musical

The correct answer is C:) International. International refers to a kind of relationship between two different countries.

50) Which of the following is NOT one of the six major learning styles?

   A) Auditory learning
   B) Speed learning
   C) Tactile learning
   D) Group learning

The correct answer is B:) Speed learning. Speed learning is not a concept in education theory, though there are practices which help make comprehension and retention more efficient and effective.

51) "A one-hundred-twenty-hour credit consisting of one-hour instructional blocks once a day, five days a week, typically over twenty-four weeks." This is the definition of

   A) A Credit unit
   B) A Carnival unit
   C) A Carnegie unit
   D) A Collision unit

The correct answer is C:) A Carnegie unit. The student hour system was made popular by the Carnegie Foundation when they used it as a requirement for their pension program.

52) What benefits can IQ tests have in schools?

   A) None, IQ tests are unreliable.
   B) None, IQ tests result in labels harmful to learning.
   C) They can be used to fire bad teachers.
   D) They can be used to help identify gifted or disabled students.

The correct answer is D:) They can be used to help identify gifted or disabled students. IQ tests can be harmful and unreliable if used incorrectly, but they can help put at-risk students on the path to the support they need.

53) What piece of legislation first mandated that schools administer yearly standardized tests?

   A) The Javits Act
   B) No Child Left Behind
   C) The Civil Rights Act
   D) None of the above

The correct answer is B:) No Child Left Behind. Standardized testing was mandated as part of the measurement system used to see if schools were meeting their Adequate Yearly Progress goals.

54) Which of the following is NOT one of the reasons standardized tests face opposition?

   A) They don't measure important traits like creativity or resourcefulness.
   B) They don't measure how satisfied students are at school.
   C) They are disproportionately hard for English language learners and students with disabilities.
   D) None of the above.

The correct answer is B:) They don't measure how satisfied students are at school. This is not a measure a standardized test would be looking for and therefore not one that they can be criticized for.

55) What legal term refers to the obligation of certain groups and individuals to act as a caring and responsible parent would when in charge of a child?

   A) In loco parentis
   B) In loco parfait
   C) In loco parenting
   D) None of the above

The correct answer is A:) In loco parentis. The term is Latin for "in place of a parent."

56) Zero tolerance policies have been shown to increase school safety and reduce violent incidents with students. True or false?

   A) True, the harsh penalties discourage students from engaging in bad behavior.
   B) False, studies have instead shown that they are not effective and might actually be harmful.
   C) Zero tolerances policies are illegal.
   D) None of the above.

The correct answer is B:) False, studies have instead shown that they are not effective and might actually be harmful. Studies that found zero tolerance policies were effective have not stood up to scientific rigor and more research has since shown them to have many negative side effects.

57) "Twenty-first-century skills" refers to what?

   A) A collection of skills needed to succeed in the information age.
   B) A collection of skills that should be taught in school.
   C) Both of the above.
   D) None of the above.

The correct answer is C:) Both of the above. Twenty-first-century skills are being advocated for by employers and education experts alike as more research shows student success in adulthood is dependent on their relationship with technology.

58) A student is assigned a research task for homework that involves finding and reporting on reliable Internet sources. They don't do the assignment because their family can't afford home Internet and they have to stay home to babysit their younger siblings. This is an example of what?

   A) The Technology Rift
   B) The Digital Fissure
   C) The Technology Divide
   D) The Digital Divide

The correct answer is D:) The Digital Divide. The student's socioeconomic situation led them to not have access to a necessary digital tool and so they couldn't complete the homework. Furthermore, their family obligations meant they couldn't make use of free public Wi-Fi somewhere else.

59) Which of the following is NOT a major drawback of e-learning?

   A) The ability to sign on whenever.
   B) The lack of immediate access to a teacher.
   C) The lack of structure.
   D) The reduced comprehension and concentration resulting from digital reading.

The correct answer is A:) The ability to sign on whenever. This is actually a benefit of e-learning, not a drawback.

60) Why might a school decide to implement a full cell phone ban?

   A) Too much screen time has been linked to poor sleep and mental health problems.
   B) Studies have shown test scores improve when cell phones are banned.
   C) All of the above.
   D) None of the above.

The correct answer is C:) All of the above. Both options listed are legitimate reasons for why a school might decide to ban cell phones, even though they are trying to help students be better digital citizens.

61) Which of the following is NOT one of FairTest's suggestions for replacing rampant standardized testing?

   A) Reduce the number and weight of standardized tests.
   B) Make colleges use alternative admissions assessments.
   C) Put more emphasis on classroom-based evidence of learning.
   D) Implement a school quality review (SQR) process.

The correct answer is B:) Make colleges use alternative admissions assessments. FairTest does not suggest making colleges use alternative methods, though many are exploring those options independently.

62) What is one way some colleges are experimenting with their admissions process?

   A) Implementing test-optional policies for applicants.
   B) Filling seats on a first-come, first-served basis.
   C) Not accepting applications every other year.
   D) Using only SAT and ACT scores when considering applicants.

The correct answer is A:) Implementing test-optional policies for applicants. Studies have shown test-optional policies increase diversity and have no effect on overall school success rates.

63) What is one suggested reason states haven't taken full advantage of the flexibility for standards in the ESSA?

   A) The ESSA is not actually that flexible.
   B) State Boards of Education are lazy.
   C) Too much bureaucracy getting in the way of adventurous and bold policies.
   D) None of the above.

The correct answer is C:) Too much bureaucracy getting in the way of adventurous and bold policies. The Bellwether report from 2017 found that a majority of state plans were unambitious and suggested part of it was the lack of incentive to try something new in a complex system.

64) What two pieces of federal legislation most significantly impacted religion in education?

   A) The Blaine Amendment, The Establishment Clause
   B) The Blaine Amendment, The First Amendment
   C) The Fourteenth Amendment, The First Amendment
   D) The First Amendment, The Equal Access Act

The correct answer is D:) The First Amendment, The Equal Access Act. The First Amendment contains the establishment clause and the Equal Access Act helps prevent discrimination against religious people.

65) In a U.S. public high school, a group of students wish to form a Bible study club to meet during lunch hours. The club would meet in the school library. Would this violate the Supreme Court rulings on religion in public schools?

   A) Yes, prayer and religious readings are not permitted in public schools due to separation of church and state.
   B) No, as the club is not mandatory for students to join.
   C) No, as long as the club meets off campus instead.
   D) There is no Supreme Court ruling around religious student clubs.

The correct answer is B:) No, as the club is not mandatory for students to join. The court ruling disallowed school mandated prayer and Bible reading but does not forbid individual religious expression and the right to association.

66) A group of Catholic parishioners approach their local public school to rent their gym for a craft sale and vigil to support a local family through a tough time. Their church recreational space is currently under renovations. The school board denies their request because they intend to pray during the event. Is this legal?

   A) Yes, prayer on school grounds is prohibited.
   B) No, this violates the Equal Access Act.
   C) Maybe, it depends on their state Blaine Amendments.
   D) None of the above.

The correct answer is B:) No, this violates the Equal Access Act. In 1984, after challenges to the Widmar ruling that allowed religious student clubs in public schools, the government said that no one could prohibit lawful access to schools based on religious affiliation.

67) A Christian private high school is refused entry into a state lottery for funds to update computer labs. What would the Supreme Court say if they challenged their state board?

   A) "The state's Blaine Amendment prohibits you from getting public funds."
   B) "The state board can do this because it can't look like it's endorsing a religious institution."
   C) "Go away, we're closed today."
   D) "Denying a generally available benefit solely on account of religious identity imposes a penalty of the free exercise of religion."

The correct answer is D:) "Denying a generally available benefit solely on account of religious identity imposes a penalty of the free exercise of religion." In 2017, the Supreme Court ruled in a Missouri case regarding funds for a playground. So long as the funds are not for religious purposes, religious schools cannot be excluded from grant programs meant to enhance student experience or learning.

68) Which of the following is NOT one of the core components of Montessori education?

   A) Montessori-trained teachers
   B) Child-directed work
   C) Uninterrupted quiet time
   D) The Multi-age classroom

The correct answer is C:) Uninterrupted quiet time. What they actually include is uninterrupted work periods.

69) Why might one Montessori school not be doing as well as another?

   A) The first school isn't using the full Montessori set of programs.
   B) The second school has a better cafeteria.
   C) Montessori programming isn't actually that successful.
   D) None of the above.

The correct answer is A:) The first school isn't using the full Montessori set of programs. A 2012 study found that schools that didn't use Montessori programming exclusively had diminished results compared to ones that did.

70) Why might a religious family choose to not send their children to their affiliated religious private school?

   A) It's too far away.
   B) It's too expensive.
   C) They're already paying for public school and don't get tax breaks.
   D) All of the above.

The correct answer is D:) All of the above. There are many reasons a parent would choose to keep their children in public school even if they would prefer a religious education, and these are some of them.

71) What is attractive about the average private school class size compared to public school?

   A) They're smaller, so there is less competition.
   B) They're smaller, which is better for student well-being.
   C) They're bigger, so children are better socialized.
   D) They're bigger, so the teachers are easier on them.

The correct answer is B:) They're smaller, which is better for student well-being. Experts agree that smaller class sizes result in students getting more individual attention and feeling more engaged.

72) When socioeconomic factors are controlled for, what do studies find about student achievement in private schools compared to public schools?

   A) The benefits of private education disappear.
   B) The benefits of private education get bigger.
   C) The benefits of private education stay the same.
   D) None of the above.

The correct answer is A:) The benefits of private education disappear. A large study from 2018 added to the evidence that there are other factors independent of private schools that affect student achievement.

73) Is it legal for a private school to gender segregate (i.e. be all girls or all boys)?

   A) No, that violates Title IX.
   B) No, that violates the Civil Rights Act.
   C) Yes, so long as they don't receive public funding.
   D) Yes, they are independent from protective legislation.

The correct answer is C:) Yes, so long as they don't receive public funding. Only publicly funded institutions are subject to Title IX compliance. However, private schools do have to follow other protective legislation.

74) A charter school can deny applications for any reason.

   A) True, they are independent and decide who to accept.
   B) False, they are publicly funded and must accept everyone.
   C) False, they have to have a good reason.
   D) None of the above.

The correct answer is B:) False, they are publicly funded and must accept everyone. However, spots are limited, so some charter schools will accept students via random lottery to stay fair.

75) A family wants to get a state voucher to send their child to a religious private school—is this legal?

   A) No, this is a violation of the Blaine Amendment.
   B) No, this violates the establishment clause.
   C) Yes, so long as vouchers are applied equally across religious and sectarian families.
   D) Yes, denying it would be a violation of the First Amendment.

The correct answer is C:) Yes, so long as vouchers are applied equally across religious and sectarian families. The Supreme Court has ruled that as long as states are granting vouchers without bias toward or against religious families, they can do so.

76) Why was Allan Bakke important to affirmative action?

   A) He led the movement to have affirmative action put in place.
   B) He was part of an initiative to have affirmative action abolished.
   C) He led a court case that prohibited diversity quotas in colleges.
   D) None of the above.

The correct answer is C:) He led a court case that prohibited diversity quotas in colleges. Allan Bakke took UC Davis Medical School to court over being denied entry twice in favor of less qualified black applicants. The courts ruled schools could no longer establish diversity quotas.

77) Opponents of affirmative action say any admissions measure that considers race violates what?

   A) Title IX
   B) The Fourteenth Amendment
   C) The Establishment Clause
   D) None of the above

The correct answer is B:) The Fourteenth Amendment. States that condone affirmative action practices might be argued to be denying equal protection and opportunity to all because of race.

78) What is mismatch in the context of affirmative action?

   A) When a student is accepted into a school too challenging for them and so they do poorly.
   B) When a student is accepted into a school they didn't apply to.
   C) When a student is accepted into a school too easy for them and they still do poorly.
   D) When a student is accepted into a program and doesn't socialize with anyone.

The correct answer is A:) When a student is accepted into a school too challenging for them and so they do poorly. These students would likely do well at another school and have a fulfilling college experience, but affirmative action put them at a disadvantage.

79) What collective trauma did the Native American populations experience up until 1978?

   A) Mass deportation
   B) Slavery
   C) Residential schools
   D) None of the above

The correct answer is C:) Residential schools. Residential schools resulted in the total erasure of much of Native American heritage and culture.

80) Why is diversity good for students?

   A) They develop better empathy.
   B) They have typically higher achievement.
   C) Their ability to think critically improves.
   D) All of the above.

The correct answer is D:) All of the above. Studies have shown in numerous educational contexts that exposure to a diverse peer group has positive effects on students, including the above.

81) Who opened the first kindergarten?

   A) Friedrich Froebel
   B) Elizabeth Peabody
   C) John Dewey
   D) Maria Montessori

The correct answer is A:) Friedrich Froebel. Friedrich Froebel opened the first kindergarten in Germany in 1837. The other answers are individuals who have had an effect on education throughout history.

82) What is homogeneous grouping?

   A) The placement of students of differing abilities into separate classrooms.
   B) The placement of students of similar abilities into separate classrooms.
   C) The placement of students of differing abilities into one classroom.
   D) The placement of students of similar abilities into one classroom.

The correct answer is D:) The placement of students of similar abilities into one classroom. This would be like having a gifted class for only gifted students.

83) What is metacognition?

   A) Thinking about one's own thinking.
   B) Thinking about others' thinking.
   C) Thinking about psychology.
   D) Thinking about strategies.

The correct answer is A:) Thinking about one's own thinking. It includes a critical awareness of oneself as a thinker and learner in order to perform better.

84) What would a proponent of charter schools say in support of keeping charter schools?

   A) They have smaller class sizes.
   B) They create competition and accountability.
   C) They are well-supported financially.
   D) All of the above.

The correct answer is D:) All of the above. Proponents would consider all of these pros of attending charter schools.

85) What are the major criticisms of IQ tests?

   A) They underestimate the contribution of factors like emotion and morality.
   B) They do not properly test for adaptive intelligence.
   C) They don't test human cognition in the way they claim.
   D) All of the above.

The correct answer is D:) All of the above. All of these are problems that people find with IQ testing.

86) Which of the following is NOT a reason that the U.S. criticizes the Japanese education system?

   A) Critical thinking is not a concept that is highly valued.
   B) Teachers have a high social status.
   C) The tendency toward rote memorization.
   D) Student mistakes can suggest the failings of the parents or community.

The correct answer is B:) Teachers have a high social status. The other answers are criticisms of the system.

87) Values-centered curriculum is characterized by what?

   A) Focusing on curriculum that adds economic value.
   B) Teaching children about the value of money.
   C) Focusing on creating "good citizens" with morals, manners, etc.
   D) None of the above.

The correct answer is C:) Focusing on creating "good citizens" with morals, manners, etc. Values-centered curriculum has nothing directly to do with finances or economics.

88) Which of the following is a disadvantage of the single salary schedule?

   A) It can foster a sense of competition between colleagues.
   B) It can put pressure on teachers to take courses they aren't passionate about.
   C) Standardized test results are one of the factors that go into teacher reports.
   D) All of the above.

The correct answer is D:) All of the above. These are all criticisms given by the National Education Association.

89) What is Bloom's taxonomy?

   A) A classification system for cognitive skills used in learning.
   B) A classification system for types of education.
   C) A classification system for different testing and their effects on secondary education.
   D) None of the above.

The correct answer is A:) A classification system for cognitive skills used in learning. Created under Benjamin Bloom's leadership, the taxonomy consists of six levels: create, evaluate, analyze, apply, understand, and remember.

90) What does the digital divide result in?

   A) Lack of expertise in coding and information technology.
   B) Unequal access to opportunities to develop skills and knowledge.
   C) An assumption that children don't need an education.
   D) None of the above.

The correct answer is B:) Unequal access to opportunities to develop skills and knowledge. Many impoverished families are unlikely to have a home internet connection, limiting opportunities school children have for education.

91) What is the responsibility of the Department of Education?

   A) Support state and local boards in their daily operations.
   B) Increase the quality of and access to education throughout the country.
   C) Oversee federal bursaries and education loans for students receiving financial aid.
   D) All of the above.

The correct answer is D:) All of the above. The current Department of Education was formed in 1980 after President Carter signed the Department of Education Organization Act in 1979.

92) Maria Montessori stressed what?

   A) The importance of respecting the classroom and its learning opportunities.
   B) The importance of respecting teachers and their ability to teach.
   C) The importance of respecting children and their desire to learn.
   D) The importance of respecting parents and their sacrifices.

The correct answer is C:) The importance of respecting children and their desire to learn. Maria Montessori put the child at the center and believed they were naturally curious and wanting to learn.

93) Why was the Committee of Ten formed?

   A) To standardize education across the country.
   B) To discuss teachers' unions.
   C) To finance the school lunch program.
   D) To designate high schools as learning institutions.

The correct answer is A:) To standardize education across the country. Some schools practiced rote memorization while others emphasized hands-on learning, so they needed something to standardize education across the board.

94) What does the term "Carnegie unit" mean?

   A) 90 hours of instruction for one hour per day, five days a week, over 24 weeks.
   B) 120 hours of instruction for one hour per day, five days a week, over 24 weeks.
   C) 150 hours of instruction for one hour per day, five days a week, over 24 weeks.
   D) 110 hours of instruction for one hour per day, five days a week, over 24 weeks.

The correct answer is B:) 120 hours of instruction for one hour per day, five days a week, over 24 weeks. This was part of the push toward educational standardization.

95) What book was a common teaching device in colonial times?

   A) Shakespeare's *Richard III*
   B) John Foxe's *Book of Martyrs*
   C) Mulcaster's *Elementarie*
   D) *The Bible*

The correct answer is D:) *The Bible*. It was broadly available and children were familiar with many of the passages.

96) What are the seven Cardinal Principles of Secondary Education?

   A) Health, command of fundamental processes, worthy home membership, vocation, civic education, worthy use of leisure, and ethical character.
   B) Health, command of fundamental processes, worthy home membership, vocation, civic duty, worthy use of leisure, and ethical character.
   C) Health, command of fundamental processes, worthy home membership, agriculture, civic education, worthy use of leisure, and ethical character.
   D) Health, command of fundamental processes, worthy college membership, vocation, civic education, worthy use of leisure, and ethical character.

The correct answer is A:) Health, command of fundamental processes, worthy home membership, vocation, civic education, worthy use of leisure, and ethical character. These specified the goals every high school should strive for.

97) How did state textbook adoption begin?

   A) In an effort to keep out anti-Confederacy messages.
   B) In a corrupt deal with publishers.
   C) To maintain open territories.
   D) None of the above.

The correct answer is A:) In an effort to keep out anti-Confederacy messages.

98) Which civil rights activist and co-founder of the NAACP wanted to end segregation and create equal opportunities for blacks through getting proper education?

A) Malcolm X
B) Martin Luther King, Jr.
C) Rosa Parks
D) W.E.B. Du Bois

The correct answer is D:) W.E.B. Du Bois. He believed that all blacks deserved equal opportunity in education.

99) The moral stages of development are associated with whom?

A) Jean Piaget
B) Lawrence Kohlberg
C) William James
D) Sigmund Freud

The correct answer is B:) Lawrence Kohlberg. His comprehensive theory of moral development is based on Jean Piaget's theory of moral judgment for children.

100) Why was the Buckley Amendment significant?

A) It protected the confidentiality of the student's educational records.
B) It provided school districts with the records of juvenile delinquents.
C) It gave impoverished families better opportunities in education.
D) It established a program for gifted students.

The correct answer is A:) It protected the confidentiality of student's educational records. It is also known as the Family Educational Rights and Privacy Act (FERPA) of 1974.

101) "In Loco Parentis" is a legal term to describe what?

    A) The legal obligation an organization has to make decisions for and regarding a child in the same way a responsible parent would.
    B) The legal obligation an organization has to make decisions for and regarding a child with a special power of attorney from the parent.
    C) The legal obligation an organization has to legally foster a child if the parent goes missing.
    D) None of the above.

The correct answer is A:) The legal obligation an organization has to make decisions for and regarding a child in the same way a responsible parent would. It also gives the responsibility of student safety to teachers.

102) Who wrote Walden Two and the Technology of Teaching?

    A) John Muir
    B) Walt Whitman
    C) Henry David Thoreau
    D) B.F. Skinner

The correct answer is D:) B.F. Skinner. He believed that the concept of free will was an illusion, and all human action was because of conditioning.

 ## Test Taking Strategies

Here are some test-taking strategies that are specific to this test and to other DSST tests in general:

- Keep your eyes on the time. Pay attention to how much time you have left.
- Read the entire question and read all the answers. Many questions are not as hard to answer as they may seem. Sometimes, a difficult sounding question really only is asking you how to read an accompanying chart. Chart and graph questions are on most DANTES/DSST tests and should be an easy free point.
- If you don't know the answer immediately, the new computer-based testing lets you mark questions and come back to them later if you have time.
- Read the wording carefully. Some words can give you hints to the right answer. There are no exceptions to an answer when there are words in the question such as always, all or none. If one of the answer choices includes most or some of the right answers, but not all, then that is not the answer. Here is an example:

    The primary colors include all of the following:
    A) Red, Yellow, Blue, Green
    B) Red, Green, Yellow
    C) Red, Orange, Yellow
    D) Red, Yellow, Blue

    Although item A includes all the right answers, it also includes an incorrect answer, making it incorrect. If you didn't read it carefully, were in a hurry, or didn't know the material well, you might fall for this.

- Make a guess on a question that you do not know the answer to. There is no penalty for an incorrect answer. Eliminate the answer choices that you know are incorrect. For example, this will let your guess be a 1 in 3 chance instead.

 ## What Your Score Means

Based on your score, you may, or may not, qualify for credit at your specific institution. The current ACE recommended score for this exam is 46. Your school may require a higher or lower score to receive credit. To find out what score you need for credit, you need to get that information from your school's website or academic advisor.

You lose no points for incorrect questions so make sure you answer each question. If you don't know, make an educated guess. On this particular test, you must answer 100 questions in 90 minutes.

Test Preparation

How much you need to study depends on your knowledge of a subject area. If you are interested in literature, took it in school, or enjoy reading then your study and preparation for the literature or humanities test will not need to be as intensive as that of someone who is new to literature.

This book is much different than the regular DSST study guides. This book actually teaches you the information that you need to know to pass the test. If you are particularly interested in an area, or feel that you want more information, do a quick search online. We've tried not to include too much depth in areas that are not as essential on the test. It is important to understand all major theories and concepts listed in the table of contents. It is also important to know any bolded words.

Don't worry if you do not understand or know a lot about the area. With minimal study, you can complete and pass the test.

We use test questions to teach you new information not covered in the study guide AND to test your knowledge of items you should already know from reading the text. If you don't know the answer to the test question, review the material. If it is new information, then this is an area that will be covered on the test but not in detail.

To prepare for the test, make a series of goals. Set aside a certain amount of time to review the information you have already studied and to learn additional material. Take notes as you study; it will help you learn the material. If you haven't done so already, download the study tips guide from the website and use it to start your study plan.

Legal Note

All rights reserved. This Study Guide, Book and Flashcards are protected under US Copyright Law. No part of this book or study guide or flashcards may be reproduced, distributed or stored in a retrieval system, or transmitted in any form or by any means, electronic, mechanical, photocopying, recording, or otherwise, without the prior written permission of the publisher Breely Crush Publishing LLC.

DSST is a registered trademark of Prometric and its affiliated companies, and does not endorse this book.

FLASHCARDS

This section contains flashcards for you to use to further your understanding of the material and test yourself on important concepts, names or dates. Read the term or question then flip the page over to check the answer on the back. Keep in mind that this information may not be covered in the text of the study guide. Take your time to study the flashcards, you will need to know and understand these concepts to pass the test.

Common schools	**Accommodation**
Advanced organizers	**Brown v. Board of Education**
Centration	**Committee of Ten**
Conservation	**Convergent thinking**

The student has had to accommodate their schema as a result of conflicting information	The use of a common space in which all students were taught provided the name
A Supreme Court battle regarding the unconstitutional nature of segregation in education	Previously learned information which can be used to help the learner understand new information
A group founded in 1982 to address problems with the U.S. high school system	The tendency of young children to focus on one aspect of a situation
Emphasizes finding the one most correct answer as quickly and accurately as possible	The ability of children to recognize that changes in shape and configuration don't necessarily indicate changes in mass or fundamental property

Cross sectional studies	**Dependent variable**
Divergent thinking	**Echoic memory**
Edgerton Bible Case	**Elaboration**
Elizabeth Peabody	**Episodic memory**

The variable which changes in response to the independent variable	When people of different ages are studied at one particular time
The recall of something that a person has just heard	Emphasizes creativity and looks for new and innovative solutions to problems
Starting with basic principles and building up to more complex ones to create an association and aid learning	Bible reading was banned because it illegally combined church and state
The recall of autobiographical facts, such as dates, places and emotions	First person to open an English-language kindergarten in the U.S.

Extinction	**Factory school model**
Formula to find out IQ?	**Iconic memory**
IDEA	**Independent variable**
Intuitive Phase (4-7 years)	**John Dewey subscribed to**

An education system that values standardized learning and tests for their efficiency in measuring achievement as well as their comparability	The weakening of a response when lack of reinforcement occurs after conditioning
The recall of something a person has seen for a brief period of time	IQ=Mental Age/Calculated Age x 100
The variable which explains the change in a dependent variable	Individuals with Disabilities Education Act Governs how states provide education for students with disabilities
Educational pragmatism	Speech becomes more social, less egocentric

Longitudinal studies	Maintenance Bilingual Education
Median	Metacognition
Mode	Most basic kind of knowledge acquisition
Pedagogy	Period of Concrete Operations (7-11 years)

Focuses on maintaining the student's primary language, while teaching them a second language as well	Where the people are followed over a long period of time and checked up on at certain points
The ability to think about thinking or control one's own thoughts	The median is the middle number in a set of data when it is organized from lowest to highest
Remembering	The number which occurs most commonly in a data set
Evidence for organized, logical thought	Methods and strategies for teaching in academic settings

Period of Formal Operations (11-15 years)	Preoperational Phase (2-4 years)
Problem-based learning	Procedural memory
Quantitative	Range
Scaffolding	Schema

Increased use of verbal representation but speech is egocentric	Thought becomes more abstract, incorporating the principles of formal logic
The recall of how to perform a specific, frequently performed task	John Dewey believed that children's interest was a key factor in learning, and PBL attempts to use the teacher's knowledge to spark interest and foster attention in the student
The difference between the highest and lowest number in a data set	The number or amount of something
A cognitive framework that helps categorize and identify concepts, experiences, and situations quickly	Materials used and resources provided (explicitly or inherently) when teaching

Semantic memory	**The Curriculum**
The Progressive Era	**Transitional Bilingual Education**
Triarchic model of intelligence	**Wait-time**
Who made the first IQ test?	**Zone of Proximal Development**

John Franklin Bobbitt	The recall of general conceptual facts which are unrelated to specific experiences
Focuses on integrating the student	A period of increase in high school enrollment between 1910 and 1940
The time between asking a question and calling on a student for the answer	Sternberg's model which claimed analytical, creative and practical factors to intelligence
Tasks that can be completed by the child, but only with the guidance of an adult or experienced peer	Alfred Binet

NOTES

NOTES

www.ingramcontent.com/pod-product-compliance
Lightning Source LLC
Chambersburg PA
CBHW081831300426
44116CB00014B/2547